D0349961

TREESTAND HUNTING STRATEGIES

BOOKS BY GARY CLANCY

White-Tailed Deer, 1991
Advanced Whitetail Hunting, 1996
Wild Turkey, 1996
Rattling Calling & Decoying, 2000
Strictly Whitetails, 2002

TREESTAND HUNTING STRATEGIES

A COMPLETE GUIDE TO HUNTING DEER FROM ABOVE

BY GARY CLANCY

The Lyons Press
Guilford, CT
An Imprint of TheGlobe Pequot Press

Copyright © 2002 by Gary Clancy

ALL RIGHTS RESERVED. No part of this book may be reproduced or transmitted in any form by any means, electronic or mechanical, including photocopying and recording, or by any information storage and retrieval system, except as may be expressly permitted by the 1976 Copyright Act or in writing from the publisher. Requests for permission should be addressed to The Globe Pequot Press, P.O. Box 480, Guilford, CT 06437.

Printed in the United States of America

Design by Compset, Inc.

10 9 8 7 6 5 4 3 2 1

The Library of Congress Cataloging-in-Publication Data is available on file.

DEDICATION

To my daughters, Michelle, Kelli Jo, and Katie, all of whom have dozens of times responded to the question, "Where is your Dad?" with a simple and honest reply of, "He is out sitting in a tree!"

CONTENTS

FOREWORD

Whenever fortunate enough to gather a captive audience, or snag some hapless individual into listening to me, I have often made the following remark:

"The thing that makes hunting so special—fishing, too, in my personal opinion—is that on any given day something can happen that you will remember for the rest of your life."

Let's face it: Very few days of our lives are like that. Sure, some big days, big moments, come and go. We all have them. But for a decent chance to paste some exciting new images in the old mental scrapbook, give me a day in the field. Give me moments like the one when I heard the sound of a stick breaking, and, looking that way, barely had an instant's vision of the biggest buck of all time leaping away, his white tail flagging. Spooked! Gone! Give me a moment like the one when the soft wet snow was sticking to everything, including my hat and jacket, and I was plodding toward the truck through the eerie quiet, giving up, heading home. Suddenly, there was a magical vision in the trail ahead. Through the big, curly, floating flakes, the image of a buck standing there looking in my direction was surreal, a picture like a painting or a dream. Somehow I managed to get the rifle up and my heartbeat rate down. I made the shot and had my buck. A small one, yes, but big enough for me and my freezer.

Most of us have such moments to remember. And those who are new to the chase will someday have theirs'. The possibilities are tremendous out there. That's why we're often so excited the night before a hunt that it's hard to turn off the switch and get to sleep.

One of the things I have always desired in a lifetime of hunting and fishing is to be afield with a companion who shares my intense feelings about what we are doing. I do not care if the person is an expert or a green beginner: I just want him to have his heart in the game. In that regard, I have been indeed fortunate to have hunted and fished with men and women, including both professional guides and personal friends, whose presence made the experience much richer than it would have been had I been alone. One such man I have wanted to hunt with for years, and somehow never had the chance, is the man who wrote this book, Gary Clancy.

You may find that to be a strange admission by someone writing an introduction to a Gary Clancy book, but bear with me and I hope you will discover that even though I have never actually hunted with Gary, I have shared his hunting experiences, observations, and knowledge on countless occasions, in print. And I know him to be a man you want to pull your chair closer to and listen up. Because when he talks about hunting, he is not giving a lecture. He will be telling you about what he saw and heard and felt. And he has seen and heard a great deal. Gary Clancy has *shaken* more dirt and snow off his boots than most other hunters have ever *walked* over.

I have been publishing Gary Clancy articles in magazines and books I have edited for so long that I really believe I have the right to be called a Charter Member of the Gary Clancy Fan Club, if not the outright Founder. The most important value an editor has is in finding things for his or her reading audience. Sure, details such as changing commas and reading proofs go with the job, but the name of the game is to put good stuff on those blank white pages. When it comes to doing just that, I have always gone with my gut feelings. The first time I read a Gary Clancy manuscript, I knew nothing whatsoever about him. But my immediate reaction was: I like this guy. I like his no-nonsense approach. I sense reliability and truth, observations I can trust. When Gary Clancy says something, he really means it. And when he doesn't know . . . well, he has the wisdom and style to say, "I don't know."

Today, thousands of Gary Clancy manuscript pages later, the proofs of this new Gary Clancy book lying on the table in front of me, my admiration of Gary Clancy's prose and trust in his reliability still are without bounds. There is only one Gary Clancy, and only he can take you to the woods and fields where he has hunted and give you the sense of being *right there.*

There is an old bromide I rather like that goes: "Give a man a fish and you feed him for a day. Teach him to fish and you feed him for a lifetime."

Gary Clancy isn't a teacher, nor does he write like one, but the end result of his prose is that you will learn a great deal from his experiences and observations. If we all had the opportunity to go on a hunting trip with Gary Clancy, we would indeed be fortunate. But the fact is that a Gary Clancy book like this one will, in the long run, prove to be far more valuable in building our personal scrapbook of memories than one hunt with Gary would have been. Armed with the insights and knowledge about treestand hunting that Gary shares with us here, we will have more than ample opportunities over the years to collect our share of trophies for the walls, the freezer, and our memories.

I mentioned that the first time I read a Gary Clancy manuscript, I did not know anything about him. That is no longer true, of course, and in reflecting on Gary's personal life, I cannot help but make the observation that a great deal of character was molded by his combat experiences in Vietnam. You can sense it in the humility and pride that show through his prose. And he is not reluctant to talk about it openly. His experiences as a "Grunt," combat infantryman, in 14 months of fighting in the jungles of Vietnam taught him a great deal about survival, teamwork, and self sufficiency. Gary Clancy did not survive jungle combat because of luck alone. He was ready, willing, and able to put up a good fight. And he did and came home.

It is Gary's belief that too many hunters are depending upon luck out there in deer country. Depending on luck and wild guesses. Guessing where the deer are, what they are doing. Guessing where to place a stand. Gary says it's time to stop letting fickle Lady Luck run your hunt and time to stop guessing. Start analyzing and thinking like a hunter, instead of standing or sitting around hoping something good will happen. Sure, this fall you'll once again hear some of those amazing stories about people who simply walk into the woods without any plan at all, sit down for a while, and end up bagging a buck big enough to get their picture in a magazine. You'll also hear stories about people winning the lottery. Forget about 'em! You've got work to do. And the real joke is that your "work"—being a real hunter instead of just wanting to bag a buck—will be far more fun than letting fate and luck deal all the cards.

With Gary Clancy as your guide, your buck hunting days are about to make a dramatic turn for the better. For openers, Gary's sheer volume of experience in a variety of deer hunting terrain, varying from his beloved Michigan forests, to Texas scrub country, to the rock-ribbed hills of the Appalachians, gives him a unique opportunity to help get you on a buck in *your* favorite area. From swamps, to cornfields, to greenfields, to pine forests, Gary Clancy knows deer country. You will begin to see the patterns of deer movements throughout their range, not as secret and mysterious events, but completely logical and quite predictable. By knowing *why* deer do the things they do, you will start developing a stronger sense of *when* they will, or will not, make their moves.

You will see that treestand hunting begins with your feet firmly planted on the ground. Finding and reading deer sign is the essential first step toward successful treestand hunting. You will learn that all deer sign is not created equal. Gary will show you exactly what you should be looking for—in all seasons and in all terrain. You will discover sign that screams, "Hunt right here!" And sign that equally screams, "Keep going! This is not the place!" And subtle sign that teases and provokes and has you questioning everything you've learned.

The woods can be empty of sign, or there can be a plethora of it—tracks, rubs, scrapes, trails, beds. What's it all mean? What's hot? What's not? You'll find the answers in this book, and you'll start feeling a strong sense of confidence about where to place your treestands.

Even then, the hunt is far from over. Choosing and using a treestand, safety considerations, best times to hunt, making the shot count: The successful treestand hunter's game plan is many-faceted and detailed. And if, as they say, "The devil is in the details," then you're going to have to hunker down and pay attention.

Even when you've done everything right in treestand hunting, even done everything by the book—Gary's book!—things can still go wrong. Even in bowhunting, but more so in gun hunting, the old problem of hunting pressure can raise its many ugly heads. Hunting pressure can definitely wreck your hunt, even your hunting vacation. But once again, Gary has alternatives. Once again he refuses to count on Lady Luck. When it comes to hunting pressure, he would ask you : "Other than worrying about it, what are you doing about it?"

I can't think of a single critical aspect of treestand hunting that Gary Clancy does not address in the pages ahead. Because of those pages, you will never go back to being a hunter who simply takes a stroll in the woods, hoping for something to happen. Your hunting will be better than ever and more fun than ever. And that's a promise!

—Lamar Underwood

Former Editor-In-Chief of *Sports Afield* and *Outdoor Life*. Editorial Director of the Outdoor Magazine Group of Harris Publications

1

HUNTING FROM A TREESTAND

M odern day deer hunters did not invent the idea of hunting game from trees. Primitive man was well aware of the advantage to be gained by being above his prospective dinner. Our ancient ancestors made good use of not only trees, but cliffs, boulders, and steeply cut river banks. When you are hunting with a club or a spear getting close takes on a whole different meaning, and ancient hunters learned in a hurry that one of the best ways to consistently get up close and personal with critters was to ambush them from above. Those who study such things remind us that if our hairy ancestors had not learned to hunt from aloft our species might have been eliminated by the very animals these men hunted.

Call it the element of surprise. I know something about that subject. Back in 1969 and 1970, I spent fourteen months as a combat infantryman in Vietnam. I was on both sides of more ambushes than I care to count. Invariably, the side that sprang the ambush won the battle.

Of course, whitetail deer do not ambush hunters. Good thing, too, or the emergency rooms would be full of gored hunters each fall. But our success does often hinge on having a deer within range that is unaware of our presence. The easiest way to consistently accomplish this goal is to hunt from a treestand.

Over the years, I've run into a few blowhards who claim that they never sit in stands or even ground blinds, but instead sneak up on their deer. Usually they go on to proclaim that sneak-hunting is the only real test of hunting skill. I do not suffer fools well and have learned to simply walk away from such opinionated bores. The truth of the matter is that even the very best sneak-hunter (still-hunter, if you insist) will quickly admit that sneak-hunting cannot hold a candle to hunting from a treestand when it comes to putting the hunter close to undisturbed deer on a consistent basis. It's that old element of surprise thing again. No matter how skillful a hunter might be at slipping through the woods, most of the whitetail deer in his path are going to sense his approach before he is within range. If this were not true, the whitetail would have been extinct long ago.

Don't get me wrong, I've got nothing against sneak-hunting. In fact, when conditions are in my favor—a favorable wind and quiet footing—I enjoy the challenge of trying to slip within range of an unsuspecting whitetail. When I occasionally pull it off, I'm quite pleased with myself, too. But when it comes to consistently seeing deer at close range and having opportunities to shoot these deer if I so choose, sneak-hunting and stand-hunting are not even in the same league. If you are going to sneak-hunt, know before you ever take that first cautious step, that most of the deer along your route are going to see, smell, or hear you before you see or hear them.

Obviously, this element of surprise is more important for bowhunters than it is for hunters using firearms. Some studies have indicated that upwards of 90 percent of all whitetail deer taken by bowhunters are taken from treestands or ground blinds. The last figures I saw from the Pope and Young Club showed that over 80 percent of all whitetails entered were taken from treestands. I've never seen any figures when it comes to gun hunters, but I would venture a guess that probably 75 percent of the millions of whitetail deer harvested during firearms seasons each year are taken by hunters on stand and that at least half of these hunters were in a treestand.

While gathering information for magazine articles, I've interviewed a lot of hunters who have been fortunate enough to take some truly outstanding bucks, and in an overwhelming majority of those hunts, the hunter was in a treestand when he took the monster buck. A couple of notable exceptions are the two largest typicals ever taken with bow and arrow: the 204 4/8-inch buck that Mel Johnson arrowed from the ground as the buck fed along the edge of a soybean field near Peoria, Illinois, back in 1965, and most recently the 208 6/8-inch Alberta monster taken by Canadian bowhunter Wayne Zaft. In Mel's case, the only reason he was not in a treestand is because they were not yet in wide use back in 1965. Zaft was not really hunting the day he encountered the giant Alberta buck. He

Hunting from a treestand often affords better shots at the animals you see.

was just out scouting and, luckily for him, he had his bow along when the big buck came ambling down the fenceline.

A treestand is so effective because hunting from an elevated position makes it more difficult for the deer to see, hear, and smell the hunter. A side benefit is that visibility is usually improved from an elevated position, making it easier for the hunter to spot approaching deer. Also, it is often possible to shoot over brush and limbs that could easily deflect an arrow or bullet fired at ground level.

There was a time, not so many years ago, when you could say with some assurance that deer never look up. Not anymore. In places where deer have been hunted from treestands for the past 30 years, deer have learned to look up. More to the point, perhaps, we hunters have trained them to look up. They do not walk around the woods with their necks craning and heads cocked skyward, but any hunter who has been treestand hunting since the 60s or 70s will tell you that deer today look up much more than did deer back then. Still, over the eons, deer have not been preyed upon from above. The main predators of whitetail deer—coyotes, wolves, and free-roaming dogs—all do their hunting from the ground. These critters are a big part of the reason why you and I find it so difficult to slip up on deer at ground level. When your life depends upon detecting predators before they are close enough to launch an attack, you either get good at it or become part of the food chain. So even though it is no longer true that deer never or seldom look up, it is still true that the odds of a deer spotting you while you are in a treestand are heavily in your favor, providing that you remain still. Deer do not see any better than we do, but when it comes to detecting motion they are masters. When you must move, do it in slow motion and preferably when the deer is behind an obstruction that blocks, or at least obscures, his vision.

You can get by with more noise aloft than you can on the ground, although I'm not sure why this is true. Maybe deer do not

Strap a portable stand to your back and you can hunt where the sign dictates.

hear as well when the sounds are above them instead of at their own level. More likely, I think, they hear the sounds, but tend to quickly dismiss noises from above that would put them on red alert if detected at ground level. A branch breaking underfoot is a good example. When attempting to sneak up on a whitetail, if you snap a branch under your boot, that deer will look up from what it is doing and instantly lock in on your position. If you freeze and hold that pose for long minutes, the deer might eventually forget about the sound it heard and go back to whatever it was doing. It is just as likely, however, that the deer will be spooked enough to simply run off or suspicious enough to circle slowly around you until it can confirm with its nose whether or not the snapping stick signaled danger. Because I am curious about such things, I have often played around with deer while seated in my treestand. (I suppose that you could call it research, but "playing around" is a term closer to the truth.) Many times, when I have had deer below my stand that I did not intend to shoot, I have used them as guinea pigs in my little experiments. This is what I have learned: If the deer below is relaxed you can snap a twig in the tree above it and about half of the time the deer will not even stop whatever it is doing. Maybe they don't hear it, but I doubt that. I just don't think a twig snapping overhead is of any concern to them. Some deer, mostly those old, nervous-ninny does, will come to attention when the twig snaps, take a quick look around, and then flick their tail and go back to munching acorns. I've chattered like a squirrel, yelped like a turkey, and cawed like a crow while perched over deer, and they have showed no concern. I've even coughed and sneezed with deer right below me and elicited either no response from the deer or, at worst, a lazy look around. A relaxed deer is much more tolerant of sounds that come from above them than they are of the same sounds at ground level. This is a huge advantage for the treestand hunter. A deer that is already nervous or suspicious is a whole different critter. Any noise, no matter how slight, no matter how common, will draw the full attention of that deer.

Relaxed or flighty, a deer will not tolerate the *clink* of an arrow making contact with an unpadded riser, the *clunk* of binoculars banging against a rifle stock, or a stand that squeaks when you shift your weight to prepare for the shot. Many hunters have learned the hard way that the mere *click* of a safety being snicked into the fire position is enough to alert a whitetail. Guard against these unnatural sounds at all costs.

Then there is the matter of smell. As long as they are down-wind of the deer, a hunter on the ground and one in a tree have the same chance of being smelled by the deer. Zero. But when a deer is upwind, the elevated hunter has the advantage. This is mainly because when a deer passes close to the tree in which the hunter is perched, even though that deer may be directly downwind of the hunter, the scent stream passes over the top of the deer. The distance at which you can hope to avoid detection by downwind deer depends upon three factors: your attempts to control human odor, what the thermals are doing at the time, and the wind. If you have showered with an unscented soap, are wearing clean clothes that have not picked up any foreign odors, or are wearing an activated-carbon suit and have sprayed your outerwear down with an odor

The rewards of hunting from a treestand.

neutralizer, you will be picked off less frequently than hunters who scoff at odor control. If the thermals are rising they will help carry your scent over the top of the deer, but if the thermals are sinking, you may be in trouble. If the breeze is blowing at a steady ten miles per hour and you are sitting 20 feet up in the tree, that breeze will likely whisk your scent right over the top of any deer passing within 20 yards of your stand. But if it is nearly calm, look out.

When the wind is blowing hard, say over 20 miles per hour, it tends to scatter your scent, making it more difficult for deer to pick up enough odor for them to get a fix on your location. I've also noticed that the longer I am in my stand, the more likely it becomes that deer will smell me. I suspect that this is because human odor starts to pool around the stand from the moment you climb up, and the longer you stay put the larger that pool of human odor becomes. It's like a drop of oil on a placid pond, it starts out small and then just keeps on spreading.

Stand-hunting will generally afford you your best shot at a deer. Most of the deer I have shot from treestands were relaxed (or at least as relaxed as a whitetail ever gets) and just doing their own thing when I dropped the string or squeezed the trigger. It is much easier to take your time, wait for the perfect opportunity, and then make a good shot at an animal that is in no hurry to go anywhere. By contrast, most of the deer I have shot at while sneak-hunting or participating in drives have been on full alert and often on the move. Sure, I have missed deer that I shot at from treestands and on occasion the arrow or bullet has not gone exactly where I planned, but my success rate is so much higher when hunting from a treestand that the two do not even invite comparison.

2

TREESTAND CHOICES

FIXED-POSITION STANDS

The fixed-position stand, which has also been called the hang-on, chain-on, strap-on, or non-climbing stand, depending on what part of the country you are from, has overtaken the climbing stand as the most popular stand with deer hunters. There is good reason for this. All but a few monster models designed to seat two hunters side-by-side are light enough that you can easily carry them to where you are going to hunt, and many models come with carrying straps. When you get to where you are going, a fixed-position stand will work on any tree sturdy enough to support your weight, regardless of the configuration or number of branches. Most of the fixed-position stands I have used over the years have been easy to hang, but even so, I always do a little backyard practice with the stand so that I'm sure that I can hang the stand quickly, quietly, and safely—even in the dark. Once it's up, if you wish, you can leave it to hunt from another time. A good fixed-position stand is solid, durable, and safe to hunt from. Another factor that has made the fixed-position stand so popular with hunters is cost. You can spend anywhere from fifty bucks to two hundred on a fixed-position stand. Because they are relatively inexpensive, many serious deer hunters own several fixed-position stands and move from one to another as conditions dictate. And although I wish it were not a factor, another advantage to a fixed-position stand is that it can easily be chained and padlocked to the tree to deter would-be stand thieves.

Nothing is perfect, though, and so it is with the fixed-position stand. It takes a number of tree steps or climbing ladders to reach a fixed-position stand situated 20 feet up a tree. Some hunters are uncomfortable making that climb. Another safety consideration is that most fixed-position stands do not feature arm rests or support rails. Hunters who are not comfortable with heights may feel insecure in a fixed-position stand, and if they do, they should not hunt from them. Hunting from a stand in which you do not feel comfortable affects your concentration and confidence, which greatly reduces the odds of your shooting a deer from that stand. You are much bet-

Credit: Ol' Man Treestands

With enough ladder or steps a fixed-position stand can be placed in any tree.

ter off hunting from a different type of stand or hunting from the ground.

CLIMBING STANDS

Some folks call these stands self-climbers, but I've never seen one climb by itself yet, so I just go with climbing stand. Climbing stands are very popular in the South and Southeast and less popular in other regions of the country, although in recent years I have seen hunters using climbing stands in areas where ten years ago you never saw one. Hunters across the nation are beginning to take notice of the advantages of climbing stands.

With a climbing stand, you eliminate the need for steps or ladders. The stand itself is your climbing tool. Since you can and should wear a safety harness while ascending and descending the tree, as well as while you are seated or standing while hunting, a climbing stand is arguably the safest stand of all. Today's climbing stands are also very comfortable and sturdy and can be made even more so with the addition of side support rails, shooting rests, and extended foot rests. Another feature you will appreciate if you happen to suffer from lower back pain or bad knees is that with a climbing stand, seat height is totally adjustable.

If you really like to get up in the air, then a climbing stand is the best option. As long as you don't run into branches that block your ascent, you can just keep on going up. Many hunters who employ climbing stands routinely hunt at 25, 30, or even 35 feet. Although height has its advantages—mainly less chance of being detected by deer—remember that the steeper the angle the smaller the kill zone becomes. If you are going to hunt from the heights then you need to practice from those same heights to insure clean kills.

Ray McIntyre, who for many years owned Warren & Sweat Treestands, hunted higher than any other hunter I have ever shared a camp with. Ray did most of his hunting in the Southeast where,

Credit: Ol' Man Treestands

Today's climbing stands are easy to use, safe, and quiet.

thanks to a preponderance of oaks, the deer have a variety of tasty acorns to choose from each fall. Each species drops at a different time, and some years one type will have a bumper mast crop while another species may experience near crop failure. Ray is a master when it comes to determining which acorns the deer are feeding on and precisely which trees the deer are spending the most time feeding under. In fact, he is the only bowhunter I've ever been in the woods with who will just flat-out ignore scrapes and rubs. When Ray finds the tree or clump of trees under which the deer have been stuffing themselves, he will take his climber, hike to the tree, and climb way up there where the buzzards perch. Ray is rarely picked off. Even deer accustomed to being hunted from above rarely look *that* high. Ray's scent is drifted well over the tops of the deer, and as I have discovered with my own experiments, the higher you go the less likely deer are to hear you or to acknowledge the small noises you do make. Opponents of hunting higher than 20 feet argue that the steeper the angle between the hunter and the target the more the kill zone shrinks. There is some truth to that, although the shrinkage is not nearly as dramatic as many assume. The key is to practice from the heights at which you are going to be hunting. Even from 40 feet up, a broadhead placed in the top third of the near lung on a deer standing 20 yards from the base of the tree will take out the off lung as well, and since the exit wound is always very low, the blood trail is usually very good and easy to follow.

One of the neat things about a climbing stand is that if you find that you need to reposition the stand to face another direction or to provide you with a better view or shooting angle, you can easily just "walk" the stand around the tree and reposition it wherever you want it. That nifty feature came into play for me just this past

Walking a climbing stand up a tree is not difficult, but it does take some practice—something you should do before the season opens.

October. I had walked the climbing stand up the tall popple (aspen) tree in the dark that morning and thought I had it positioned perfectly so that I could get a shot at any deer using either the main trail 15 yards from the base of the tree or the secondary trail 10 yards beyond the first trail. But right at first light, a coyote came slinking down the secondary trail, and I realized as I watched the predator silently ghost by that the stand was in the wrong position for affording a good shot to that trail. I simply walked the stand a third of the way around the tree to the left and now had both trails lined up for good shots from both sitting and standing positions. An hour later a family group of seven does and fawns came slowly ambling along that secondary trail and I put one of my management tags on the old gal in the lead. I would not have had a shot without the ability to quickly and quietly adjust my position.

The biggest drawback to a climbing stand is that it cannot be used in trees with low branches. A few small branches can be trimmed as you climb, but too many branches or branches too large to be quickly sawed through with a small hand saw preclude the use of a climbing stand. It's true that in some parts of the country, like where I live in southeastern Minnesota, there are far more trees better suited for fixed-position stands than for climbing stands. However, even here in the Midwest, perhaps the major stronghold of the fixed-position stand, I find myself using a climber on an increasing number of hunts each season. It's surprising how many trees you can find that are suitable for a climbing stand when you are really looking for them.

A few years ago I would have listed noisy, heavy, cumbersome, and awkward to carry as drawbacks of the climbing stand, but I really cannot say that about the new breed of climbing stands. Treestand manufacturers have listened when hunters have told them they want climbing stands that are lightweight, compact, and easily transported with backstraps. They have heeded our pleas for climbing stands that do not rattle, clink, clank, and clang as we climb. There are still some real dogs out there, but most of the climbing stands on the market today are a huge improvement over the climbing stands many of us grew up using.

It still takes some physical agility and strength to get a climbing stand into position, but you certainly do not have to be a 20-year-old hardbody to use a climbing stand. Only you can make the final determination as to whether or not you have the coordination, agility, and strength necessary to use a climbing stand. If you are concerned about it, try a buddy's climber before you plunk down dollars for one of your own.

From September until sometime in January, there are always two stands in the bed of my pickup. These are my emergency stands. One of them is a climbing stand.

LADDER STANDS

Ladder stands are becoming more popular, it seems, with each passing year. Part of the current appeal of ladder stands is that they are safe, sturdy, and easy to climb. This makes them a logical choice for older hunters, and if the average age for hunters keeps going up instead of down, you will see increasing use of ladder stands in years to come. Not that ladder stands are used exclusively by older hunters, but they are certainly a favorite with the gray whisker set. Comfort seems to become more of a factor as a hunter ages and a good ladder stand is about as comfortable as you can get in the woods without nailing your La-Z-Boy recliner to a tree.

I've hunted out of a lot of ladder stands over the years. My personal point of view is that they are excellent tools for the gun hunter, especially when they are set up in locations that allow for good visibility and fairly long-range shots. A good ladder stand is as solid as a '56 Buick and when you couple that all-important feature with padded rails on which to rest your rifle, sniping a whitetail feeding in a green field at 150 yards is a "gimmee" for most deer hunters.

Although I have shot a few deer out of ladder stands while bowhunting, it is not my first choice, and I never set up a ladder stand and hunt out of it that same day as I so often do with a climbing stand or a fixed-position stand. Deer notice ladder stands, and in order for a ladder stand to be effective for the bowhunter, it must be in position long enough for the deer to become accustomed to its presence. I do not know how long it takes for a deer to accept a ladder stand as just another part of its environment. My guess is that it varies from deer to deer. Young deer probably give the ladder a cursory sniff and go right on about their business. Older does might well walk out of their way for weeks to bypass a newly-positioned ladder stand and a mature buck may never totally accept the stand.

The acceptance factor is also greatly influenced by how often the stand is hunted. While hunting on plantations and hunt clubs in the Southeast, where ladder stands are very common, I have watched deer step cautiously out of thick cover and into a green

This ladder stand is well camouflaged.

field and then stare for long minutes at each of the several ladder stands that surround the field. These deer know that if a stand is occupied they are in danger.

When I erect a ladder stand for use either for gun hunting, bowhunting, or both, I take the time to brush it up. I wire branches to the trunk of the tree that the base of the stand is strapped or chained to. These branches will help to break up my outline when I am in the stand and will allow me to get by with some movement. I also wire branches to the shooting rails and to the outside edge of the stand platform. I even take the time to wire branches along the outside rails of the ladder. All of this helps to make the stand less obvious. I'm not fooling myself. I know that the deer frequenting the area are still going to find the stand and check it out, especially at night when deer do a lot of snooping around, but it seems to me that deer accept a well-brushed ladder stand quicker than they do one left exposed. And I'm convinced that when the rut is on and a big bruiser from the next township comes cruising through looking for a hot doe a ladder stand I've taken the time to brush up is less likely to catch his eye than one devoid of any camouflage other than paint.

TRIPOD STANDS

Much of the hunting I've done in Texas has been from tripod stands. Most feature three legs (a few have four) and a stand platform with a swivel seat and support bars that double as a rifle rest when the time comes. These stands are popular in Texas because in many parts of the state trees big enough to support a fixed-position stand or a climber are in very short supply. But you can take a tripod stand, back it into a clump of mesquite, cut mesquite branches to wire to the platform and support bars, and presto, you've got yourself an elevated stand. Although a tripod stand is better suited to the rifleman, I have bowhunted from one on several occasions. In fact, I may be the only hunter living in Minnesota who owns a tripod stand. I keep one down in the shed because sometimes I run into situations where no other stand will do the job. I've used the tripod stand along brushy fencerows, in wild plum thickets, cattail and phragmite sloughs, and in second-growth cutovers. Anyplace where you need to get elevated but do not have the trees to do the job is a good bet for a tripod stand.

Even though I brush in the tripod stand, I like to give the deer plenty of time to get accustomed to the presence of the stand before I hunt it. This is not so important if you are hunting with a rifle while overlooking a big cutover, but it is vitally important if you are hunting with stick and string.

A good tripod stand is expensive to manufacture and that cost is passed along to you. But if you are going to invest in a tripod stand, I

Tripod stands are more common in the Texas brush country than anywhere else I have ever hunted.

encourage you to spend the money to get a good one. A cheap tripod stand is nothing but junk. I've had the wind topple two of them—while I was in them. That's a thrill I can live without.

Most tripod stands are ungainly, heavy, and bulky, and it takes two men to do a good job of setting one up. Trying to do it yourself will only lead to frustration.

There is no doubt that the tripod stand is very much a "specialty stand," but when you run into a situation where you need one you will realize that no other stand could get the job done.

PERMANENT STANDS

Most articles and books dealing with treestand hunting simply dismiss permanent stands as unsafe and unsightly and leave it at that. I won't, because while I agree with the unsightly part (I've yet to see a permanent stand that added anything to the beauty of the woods), the safety part is another issue. I maintain that a well-constructed and well-maintained permanent stand is as safe as any fixed-position, climber, tripod, or ladder stand ever built, and in some cases, they are safer.

My friend Mike Pavlick runs Golden Triangle Whitetail Outfitters in western Illinois. While he uses many fixed-position portable stands on the thousands of acres he owns or leases, Mike also has constructed dozens of permanent stands for his guests.

"Let's face it," Mike says, "the hunting population is not getting any younger. Many of my hunters are in their 50s, 60s, and 70s. While some of these guys are still in excellent shape, others are not, and they find climbing into a portable stand difficult. Many of them also find it difficult to sit comfortably in a portable stand for any length of time. Most of my hunters prefer to hunt from one of my permanent stands."

Mike does not spare any expense in the construction of his permanent stands. He uses treated lumber, lag screws instead of nails wherever possible, and 2×6s instead of 2×4s at all stress points. His stands are rock-solid, roomy, and comfortable enough to make all day sits a pleasure instead of a torture test. Each stand is inspected prior to the new season and any necessary repairs made. If the tree itself has become damaged in a storm or by disease, the stand is moved to another location.

Before you rush out to build a permanent stand, be sure to check the regulations. Permanent stands are not legal on most public land. If you are fortunate enough to hunt private property with the permission of the landowners, check with them before building a stand.

Personally, although I find a good permanent stand to be safe and comfortable, I rarely hunt out of one because I am convinced that some deer, most notably mature deer, just never fully become comfortable with going near a permanent stand. I know that there

This stand, which I hunted out of in Saskatchewan, does not look like much, but it was actually very safe and quite comfortable.

have been a lot of very big deer shot from permanent stands, but I remain convinced that unless a big buck is being pressured or being led by the nose by a doe in heat he will usually detour around a permanent stand. This is, of course, a much larger consideration when hunting with a bow than with a gun.

Never—no matter what—climb into a permanent stand you happen to come across while in the woods. Unfortunately, legally or illegally, many hunters build permanent stands and then abandon them after a year or two. You have no way of knowing the condition of that stand. All it takes is one loose nail or one rotten board to end your hunting for that day and maybe forever.

JUST A TREE

The first treestand I ever used for deer hunting was just a tree. In fact, I would guess that I hunted from branches in trees for a half-dozen years before I set foot on the platform of what we know today as a treestand. It may sound primitive now, but actually hunting from a tree without the use of a stand has some advantages. You don't have to lug anything into the woods with you. Before there was such a thing as a screw-in step I used to carry a 30-foot piece of rope in my fanny pack. When I found a tree I wanted to climb, I simply threw the rope over the lowest sturdy branch and pulled myself up. When screw-in steps became available, I carried two or three of them in my fanny pack. Two or three steps was usually plenty to allow me to reach the lowest branch and pull myself up. The trick was to find a tree with sturdy, semi-horizontal limbs. White oaks, and to a lesser extent red oaks, often display this configuration, as do some species of maple. I've also hunted while standing on the branches of willow, cottonwood, basswood, elm, and box elder.

Hunting from the branches is a sneaky way to hunt. No chains to rattle, no stand to squeak. No working up a lather just putting up the stand or walking it up the tree. Deer are less likely to see you

This hunter found a comfortable stand among the branches of a tree.

because there is no platform, no ladder, no steps. And other hunters can't pinpoint your hunting hotspots.

It may sound strange, but even though I own a couple dozen treestands, I still find myself hunting from branches every so often. There is a small woodlot a few miles south of my home where I have permission to hunt. The first year I hunted there, which was only two years ago, I was walking along the south edge of the woods looking for a good place to hang a fixed-position stand for the evening hunt. It was the first week of bow season and I was betting that the deer were still feeding on the unharvested soybeans that abutted the woods. When I found a good trail leading out into the soybeans I started looking for a suitable tree in which to hang the stand. Instead, my eye fixed on a big oak that had been snapped in two by a strong wind that had roared through the area early that summer. The tree had snapped about twelve feet above the ground, but it had not snapped cleanly. The point where the tree had broken made a perfect natural treestand. I only needed to use two screw-in steps to reach the first of several branches that allowed me to slip easily into position. The first deer to venture out along the trail later that evening was a small seven point buck. I let him walk by, hoping that we might meet again in a couple of years. Ten minutes after the little buck had made his appearance I heard a twig snap back in the woods. I slipped my release onto the string and got ready. The first deer was a button buck, the next probably his sister. I figured the next one would be a mature doe and it was. She was eight steps away from the base of that wind-toppled oak when I sent the broadhead through her lungs. I've since shot two other deer from that same tree.

Hunting from branches has its drawbacks, too. While some branches are more comfortable than others, I've never found any yet that were as comfortable as a regular treestand. Most of the time you are going to have to stand, although when I hunted from the branches more often, I used to carry one of those screw-in or strap-on portable seats so that I could at least give my legs and feet a rest once in awhile. I also used to carry what was commonly called a crotch-stand. My first one was an eighteen-inch long section of 2 × 6 with a V-cut in each end. You jammed that board down into a crotch and it gave you a place to stand or sit. I later bought one that was made of steel and folded up. Back when I was young, I often spent long hours—and sometimes all day—standing on branches. I would not want to do that anymore. Nor would I think of hunting from branches without a safety harness.

If the bark is wet or covered with snow or ice, don't even think about hunting from branches. It is tough enough standing on a branch and shifting around to get in position for a shot when the branches are dry; you are asking for a fall if the bark is wet.

3

TREESTAND SAFETY

I've never been big on rules. In fact, my mother was fond of saying that the old cliche, "rules are meant to be broken," was written just for me. So let's call the following "safety suggestions" instead of rules; suggestions that can save a lot of pain and maybe even your life.

Suggestion 1. Never attempt to climb into or out of a stand with your gun or bow. No, I don't care if it is slung over your back. Use a rope to pull the gun or bow up after you are settled in your stand and to lower the gun or bow before you climb down.

Suggestion 2. Unload your gun before you pull it up or lower it from your stand. Think how silly you are going to feel if you shoot yourself with your own gun.

Suggestion 3. Do not leave portable treestands in place from one season to the next. This is especially critical with stands that have wooden platforms or that are attached to the tree with straps or rope. Rotted wood or a strap or rope weakened by exposure to the elements can easily break.

Suggestion 4. Always wear a full-body safety harness. Always.

Suggestion 5. Don't skimp on the tree steps. Use enough steps so that you do not have to wonder where the next step is when climbing down.

Suggestion 6. Put an extra tree step above the stand so that you can grab it when stepping onto the stand. Many hunters have fallen when trying to use the stand itself or the strap or chain to help hoist themselves aboard the stand.

Suggestion 7. If you are afraid of heights, don't force yourself to hunt from a treestand. You cannot enjoy the hunt, concentrate, or shoot decently when your main concern is falling. Think about hunting from ground blinds.

Suggestion 8. I would suggest that you never use tree limbs as steps, but nobody is going to listen to that advice, so just be very careful in choosing only the sturdiest branches. And remember, just because a branch held your weight last season, does not mean it will do the same this year. My brother-in-law found this out the hard way, and we carried him out of the woods strapped to a sheet of plywood. Also, remember that limbs break easier in cold weather than in warm weather.

Suggestion 9. Never trust a tree step that has been left in the tree from one season to the next. Constant exposure can cause the step itself to stress and crack, but more commonly the wood rots around the screw threads and the step pulls out when you put your weight on it.

Suggestion 10. When using screw-in tree steps, make sure that you are seating them in solid wood and not punky or rotting wood. Also, be very careful of thick-barked trees like old oaks and giant cottonwoods. The thick bark makes it difficult to get into the meat of the tree for a secure grip.

Be especially vigilant when using screw-in steps on trees with thick bark, such as mature cottonwoods. It is very easy to get a bite into the bark but not the meat of the tree.

Suggestion 11. Always wear a climbing belt when erecting climbing ladders or sticks.

Suggestion 12. Inspect all of your stands before the season. This is especially crucial if you hunt from wooden permanent stands. I have found stress fractures, popped rivets, and missing bolts during my pre-season inspections of commercial stands, as well.

Suggestion 13. If you think a stand is unsafe, don't use it. Period.

Suggestion 14. Be extra careful in your stand and climbing into and out of your stand if it is wet from snow, ice, or rain. Rubber boots, worn by most bowhunters, are especially treacherous on wet surfaces.

Suggestion 15. Always practice putting up a fixed-position stand, or climbing with a climbing stand, before the actual hunt. There is nothing more frustrating than banging and clanging around in the dark trying to hang a stand or climb up a tree. It's dangerous too.

Suggestion 16. A climbing stand and a smooth-barked tree, especially if that bark is wet, can spell trouble. Use extra caution.

Suggestion 17. If a storm with strong winds and/or lightning moves in, get down from the stand. I did not follow my own advice last season and had lightning strike and shatter a tree just 200 yards from where I perched. The scariest part was that I had just hung a stand in the tree the lightning hit and had planned to hunt from it that day, but a switch in the wind forced me to hunt the other stand.

Suggestion 18. If you do fall from a stand with your gun or bow in your hands toss them as far away from you as you can. Landing on them only increases the likelihood of injury.

Suggestion 19. I've often read that if you get drowsy while on stand you should climb down and stretch out on the ground or go back to camp or your vehicle for a nap. If I did that every time I got sleepy, I would never get a deer. Instead, I carry an extra safety belt in my fanny pack and when I feel the nods coming on I sit down, strap the safety belt across my chest, cinch myself tight to the tree, and take a little snooze. Between that tightly-cinched safety belt and the full-body safety harness

I wear, I figure I'm probably safer than I am in my own bed. I do wonder, though, how many bucks have tiptoed past my stand while I've been grabbing 20 winks!

Suggestion 20. It helps if someone knows where you are hunting and when you plan to return. If you don't show up somebody will become concerned and will know where to look for you. These days, carrying a cell phone in your pocket is cheap insurance. Unless you are dead, you can call for help.

Never climb into or out of your stand with your gun or bow. Use a rope to raise and lower your weapon.

AFTER THE SHOT

Joe was only in his second season of bowhunting when he took the fall. During his first season he had shots at a doe and a small buck, but got so excited that he missed them both. He was determined not to let that happen again. The next time he got the opportunity at a deer, he continually told himself, he was going to pick a spot, make a smooth release, and watch that arrow fly true to the target, just like he did when practicing in his backyard.

It was cool, that November morning, but not too cold. Just about perfect, Joe figured. But by midmorning Joe had not seen a single deer. He was surprised at that, but not concerned. In the dark that morning he had heard two bucks fighting just down the ridge from his stand. He had never heard or seen bucks fighting before and just listening to the two bucks go at it had been a treat. Joe was sure that one of the bucks would come his way after the battle was over, but it didn't happen. He was not discouraged, though. The rut was coming on and the ridge was pockmarked with fresh scrapes. From his stand, Joe could see a string of gleaming rubs, with some of the rubs on the larger trees that the big boys like to work. With plenty of lunch packed and a bottle of water, he was determined to hunt all day.

Just before noon, Joe thought he heard a buck grunt behind him. He listened hard and, sure enough, he heard the buck grunt again. Standing slowly, he plucked his bow off of the hook and turned slightly in the stand so that he could see behind the sturdy oak to which his stand was lashed. What he saw instantly turned his knees to jelly. A big buck, at least a ten pointer and probably more, was making his way down the ridge. As Joe watched in slack-jawed amazement, the buck worked a scrape, first hooking his antlers into the overhanging branch, then rubbing his face slowly along the drooping branch for what seemed like several minutes. Then the buck squeezed his hind legs together, squatted slightly, and urinated in the scrape. Joe had read about bucks working scrapes before, but he had never seen it with his own eyes. When the buck finished, he began walking slowly and deliberately towards Joe's stand again, but at 50 yards the big buck stopped to work over a cedar that already showed scars from previous years. The buck didn't fool around. He leaned heavily into the tree, jerking his head up and down, twisting his nut-colored rack in the green branches, which soon littered the forest floor. Joe was surprised at the viciousness of the attack. When the buck finished with the tree, he stepped back and stood there for a few long moments, as if admiring the job he had done. Then he turned and started walking downhill. Joe frantically dug inside his jacket for his grunt call. Putting the call to his lips, he tried to blow a soft grunt, but the noise that came out the end of the tube sounded more like a strangled duck. No matter, the buck walking in the noisy carpet of leaves never heard it and just kept on walking. Now really panicking, Joe blew harder on the call. This time the buck heard the sound and stopped in mid-stride, swiveling his head from side to side, ears cupped as he tried to get a fix on the location of the sound he had heard. Joe grunted again and the buck never hesitated. Ears laid back, the buck marched steadily towards the oak in which Joe perched. All of the blood in his system seemed to rush to his temples, where it pounded like the rush of ocean surf. Joe's right leg began to bounce and the bow shook in his hands. As the buck came ever closer, Joe took one last deep breath and, afraid that the buck might detect his labored breathing, held his breath under the face mask. The buck stepped behind a screen of scrub red oak and stopped. Now only 20 yards away but with its vitals obscured, the buck stood, nose high, searching the wind for its ancient message. Seconds dragged by. Joe, out of breath, had to gulp for air. The buck turned and seemed to look up in the tree and Joe was sure it was over, but just as quickly the buck lowered his head to the ground, sniffed something, and then took a step that put his chest in the clear. Joe drew, and when the sight pin wobbled across the buck's chest, Joe dropped the string and sent the arrow on its way. As the sharp broadhead slipped neatly through the top of its heart the buck instinctively kicked out with both hind legs and bolted off the ridge. It was a short run. From his stand high in the oak, Joe could see the buck suddenly go down on his nose and flip end over end on the steep slope. He let out a wild whoop of pure glee and stepped off of the stand into space.

Joe was lucky. He was hunting with a buddy who knew where his stand was located, and when Joe did not return to the vehicle by an hour after dark, his buddy went looking for him. He found Joe, with both legs and his back broken, lying where he had landed under the tree. At first, doctors did not think Joe would walk again, but now, ten years after that fall, Joe is able to get around with a cane. He hunts from a ground blind now and uses a crossbow because his smashed right shoulder never healed strong enough to allow him to shoot a bow.

You might think it silly that anyone would just step off of a treestand into space, but Joe's case is not unusual. Lots of hunters have done the same thing. Most were smart enough to wear safety belts, but as one hunter who has done it told me, "You tend to forget about that belt when you take that fateful step into nothing but air."

A national survey revealed that the most common time for a hunter to take a fall is after he has shot a deer and is getting ready to climb down or is in the act of climbing down from the stand. The problem, of course, is adrenaline. Most of us get excited when we see a deer approaching our stand. We get even more excited if it is a deer that we would like to shoot. If the deer happens to be a dandy buck, the excitement level goes right off the charts. If everything goes well and we actually get a shot and connect, the adrenaline spikes. This is not a good time to attempt to climb down from the stand. Stay put.

If you miss, there is no advantage in climbing down from your stand. Just sit still and watch. Many times a deer that has been missed, especially with an arrow, will return—probably out of curiosity. Or there may be another deer nearby that you have not seen. Even if you think you might have hit the animal but are not sure, wait a half-hour before climbing down to check for blood. If you are sure that the hit was good, or even if you saw the animal go down, resist the urge to immediately scramble to the ground. Give yourself time to calm down. The deer is not going anywhere.

Look closely and you will see that I am wearing a full-body safety harness. You won't find me in a treestand without one. I don't ever plan to fall again, but I know that if I do the full-body harness will break my fall without injuring or killing me.

The worst thing that you can do, regardless of what happens after you take the shot, is to rush down from your stand. Bad things happen when you get in a hurry 20 feet off the ground.

WHY I WEAR A FULL-BODY HARNESS

Remember the Great Halloween Ice Storm of 1991? I sure do. I was stubborn and stupid enough to be sitting in a portable treestand lashed to the trunk of a big oak on a ridge down near Lanesboro that day. I knew that when the rain started freezing as soon as it touched anything I should try to carefully climb down from my treestand while I still had a chance of making it to the ground in one piece. I knew that I should not continue to hunt, but the deer went crazy that afternoon. The critters knew that there was a bad storm brewing and they were out in force, chowing down just in case they were forced to lay low for a day or two. The bucks were feeling pretty rammy by the end of October, anyway, so between mouthfuls of whatever they could find, they would chase a doe or two around. It was quite a circus. Maybe, if not for the big ten pointer I had missed on opening day of bow season from a stand just a few hundred yards away, I would have had the good sense to climb down while I still could. But down in my hunter's gut I *knew* that with all of the deer activity I was seeing that afternoon, it was only a matter of time before the big buck made an appearance. So instead of doing what I knew I should do, I hung onto that rocking, ice-caked oak and waited.

Finally, late that afternoon, the big buck made his appearance. He was to my right, and being right-handed I had to stand to try to make the shot. When I stood, my feet went out from under me and I found myself suddenly hanging in midair, my safety belt snugged tightly just below my ribs. I drew on the big buck as I swayed back and forth at the end of that safety belt, but when I got the string back I realized that the arrow had been dislodged by the force of the fall and had tumbled to the ground. All I could do was hang there in the driving, freezing rain and watch the big buck walk out of my life forever.

I nearly died hanging there on the end of that safety belt. Everything was so slippery I could not get back into my stand, and the belt, cinched tightly right below my heart, was literally squeezing the life out of me. Finally, when I was about gone, I somehow managed to heave myself back onto the stand. After resting a few minutes, I began to climb down. The tree steps were like Popsicles, and I had only made it a few feet when I lost my grip and fell. I landed on my back and thought I had broken it, but I was lucky and just had the wind knocked out of me.

A day or two later I was back in a treestand, but this time — for the first time — I was wearing a full-body harness. I've probably spent nearly 1,000 days in a treestand since then, and each time I'm wearing a full-body harness. I have not fallen since that Halloween day in '91 and I hope I never do, but I know that if I do someday take a fall my full-body harness will save my life, not take it. You can't say the same about a safety belt.

Plenty of hunters have been injured or even died as a result of a safety belt. Most are asphyxiated when the belt cinches around their chest as mine did that Halloween day. Others have hung upside down after a fall and have lost conciousness. Some do a dramatic flip when they hit the end of the safety belt and break their backs. Still others have slipped right out of the belts and been killed or injured when they hit the ground.

A safety belt is better than nothing, but it is a poor substitute for a full-body harness. The kind of harness I'm talking about has industrial strength straps that secure around your shoulders, waist, and legs. I've tested several makes of full-body harnesses in the backyard by securing a treestand a few feet off the ground, climbing aboard, securing the harness properly to the tree, and jumping off the stand. In every case the impact of my fall was absorbed by my entire body, which is precisely what the full-body harness is designed to do. It's also important to note that climbing back into the stand while wearing a full-body harness is much easier than when dangling from a safety belt.

An added feature of a full-body harness, that I make good use of dozens of times each season, is that it doubles as a climbing belt. You can attach the climbing strap to the tree and slide it along as you climb up or descend. If I had been using one during that ice storm, I would have been spared a nasty fall. I also use mine all of the time when hanging stands, and it makes that job so much easier. Simply attach the climbing strap to the tree and, instead of hanging on by one hand or sometimes just with your legs, you now have both hands free to work with the stand.

Several of the big treestand companies have taken the expensive step of providing a full-body harness with each stand they sell. I personally applaud Summit, API, and Ol' Man Treestands for leading the way. I hope that every treestand manufacturer follows their lead.

But don't wait until you buy a new treestand to upgrade from a safety belt to a full-body harness. Make it your next outdoor purchase. I've worn full-body harnesses from Ol' Man, Rutherford Outdoors, and the well-respected Seat-O-The-Pants harness from Fall Woods and can vouch for them all. A good one will set you back 50 to 60 bucks, but isn't your life worth that much?

4

A GAME PLAN FOR EARLY SEASON WHITETAIL

Most bowhunters of my acquaintance are one-dimensional hunters when it comes to the early season. The only game plan most of them have is to hunt deer coming to fields or clearcuts. Hey, it's a good plan for as long as it lasts, but in most cases, it is not going to last long. Deer, especially mature bucks and does, are quick to pick up on the fact that they are being hunted. Once that happens, you can forget about taking a mature deer on a field or clearcut. This leaves you with a couple of choices: You can hang up your bow for a month or so and wait for the rut to kick in, or you can put together a game plan that will allow you to squeeze a lot more action out of those early weeks of the season.

Here is the game plan I use. You are welcome to copy it, modify it to fit your own style, or ignore it and stay home and clean the garage and rake leaves while I go hunting. The choice is yours.

GETTING THE MOST OUT OF A FIELD

All summer deer filter out into fields and clearcuts in the evening to feed. When the bow season opens, hunters are waiting in stands on the edges to take advantage of the situation. If you connect on that first evening, there is no problem, but if you do not, you now have to figure out how to get down out of that treestand without alerting every deer in the field to your presence. If you spook the deer, there will be fewer deer in the field during shooting light the next evening. If you spook them again the next evening, the field will still be vacant when darkness settles in on the third evening. The keys to getting the most out of your early season fields or clearcuts are: (1) Have more than one stand on a field so that you will not be inclined to hunt a stand when the wind is wrong. (2) Try to have more than

Tiffany Profant with her first buck by bow. The early season is a great time to introduce youngsters or new hunters to the sport because the weather is comfortable and you will usually see plenty of deer.

one field to hunt. (3) Be sure you can get into your stand without alerting deer that will later be using the field. If you cannot, forget that stand site. (4) Consider using a ground blind instead of a tree-stand. A ground blind, either a commercial pop-up type blind or a blind crafted from native materials, is often easier to slip into and vacate without being detected. If you are going to use a ground blind, it should be in place well before the season so that deer become accustomed to its presence. (5) If you can arrange it, have someone drive into the field (with the landowner's permission, of course) and pick you up at or near your stand. When the vehicle arrives the deer will temporarily scatter off the field, giving you time to climb down from your stand and get back to the vehicle without alerting deer to your presence. I've hunted the same field for over a week just by employing this tactic. (6) Never attempt to hunt a field or clearcut in the morning. The only thing you will accomplish is to ruin your chances for the evening.

WHEN THE ACTION ON THE FIELD DRIES UP

Eventually, no matter how careful you are, deer are going to catch on and the evening action on the field will dry up. Deer don't quit feeding in the field, they adjust their feeding schedule, which simply means that they do not enter the field until after shooting hours have expired. But the interesting thing is that they still tend to get up out of their beds at the same time each day. Instead of trucking straight to that favorite field or clearcut, they tend to mosey along, browsing here and there, taking their sweet old time, and then hanging back from the field just killing time waiting for darkness. Some guys call them staging areas, others call them transition zones. Whatever you call them, these are the places to hang your stand when the action on the field ceases. Look 50 to 100 yards back off the edge of the field. Look for trails, rubs, and signs of browsing.

SPEAKING OF RUBS

Speaking of rubs, I am amazed at how many bowhunters still lump rubs, scrapes, and the rut all into one neat little package. The truth is that rubs are the best early season buck sign you can find. The rubs you find early are rubs made by the dominant buck in the area. Little bucks don't start doing their thing until later in the fall. That's why I spend a lot of time looking for and following rub lines during the early weeks of the season. Find a good rub line and you have found the number one location in the woods for a crack at Mr. Big. (This will be discussed in greater detail in a later chapter.)

THEN THERE ARE ACORNS

Most of us tend to assume that when deer vacate fields it is due to hunting pressure. Often it is, but just as often you can blame acorns. Whitetail deer are bonkers over acorns. The early weeks of the season will frequently coincide with the time when acorns are dropping. When this happens, deer are often so busy scarfing up acorns in the woods that they don't get out to the fields or the clearcut until well after dark, sometimes not at all.

I have a little spot over in western Wisconsin that is a perfect example. It's a flat, probably ten acres in size, and it is studded with giant white oaks. Deer bed on the high ridge above the little flat and make their way across in late afternoon on their way to feed in the soybean, alfalfa, and corn fields down below. I have a couple of stands on the flat to intercept them as they move through. But when the acorns start dropping fast, usually mid-September to early October in this neck of the woods, the deer don't just move through, they congregate on that little flat to munch acorns. If I did not know about that little flat and the acorn connection, I would still be sitting on one of my stands along the edges of those fields wondering what happened to all of the deer.

This beautiful Manitoba buck was taken by Jim Hanson on the first day of September. Manitoba and North Dakota are two places where a bowhunter can find a buck in velvet during the first week of the season.

By the way, the best way to prepare for the acorn drop is to know in advance which trees are loaded with mast. I visit my hunting areas in late summer armed with a pair of good binoculars and search the tops of the oaks for clusters of acorns. When I find a tree, or better yet a group of oaks, loaded with acorns, I prepare a stand site; if I am on private land, I go ahead and hang a stand or two.

DEER LIKE TO DRINK, TOO

For many years, like most deer hunters I know, I never gave much thought to where deer drink. But in the last few years I've given this a lot of attention and it has paid big dividends. Early in the season, the weather is often very warm and deer need to drink. They will usually tank up in the morning before bedding down for the day and will then drink again in late afternoon when they get up. If it is very warm, they will sometimes slip away for a drink at midday.

The best situations for hunting near water occur where water sources are scarce. This concentrates deer at the available water source and can lead to lots of action. In many prime whitetail habitats, though, there is so much water available that hunting over it would appear to be a waste of time. I say "appear to be," because I have noticed over the years that even when water is readily available at a number of different locations deer, like some people, have favorite watering holes. In the case of whitetail deer, the key is seclusion. Deer may drink from that clear, cool stream trickling through the pasture at night, but you won't catch them drinking there during shooting hours. Instead, they will take their drink from that scummy, stagnant pond back in the woods, the one almost choked by briars and vines. Find a secluded pond or spring seep back in good whitetail habitat and I'll bet you will find the soft earth along its edges littered with deer tracks.

BYE-BYE BUGS

You know what I really hate? Sitting in a treestand waiting for a deer while skeeters, gnats, and flies feast on me. Let's face it, biting insects tend to take the fun out of the experience. Insect repellants help, but deer can smell that stuff a mile away. A better solution is an insect-proof suit. The best I have found is made by Bug Out. Pants, jacket, hood, and gloves roll up in a small stuff sack that takes up little room in your fanny pack and weighs next to nothing. Bug Out suits are available at most major sporting good outlets. If you can't find one near you, call 877-928-4688, or check them out on the Web at www.Bug-Out-outdoorwear.com.

5

THE PRESSURE FACTOR

A lot of hunters spend too much time complaining about other hunters, bemoaning the fact that they must share the woods with other hunters and eventually blaming others for their lack of success. But hunting pressure is a fact of life on opening weekend of the firearms deer season. Unless you are fortunate enough to own your own land and are selfish enough to not share it with family members or friends, you are not likely to be the only hunter in a chunk of timber on opening day. Even if you do have some property pretty much to yourself, hunting pressure on adjacent lands will greatly influence your success.

I've often read that the best remedy for dealing with opening day hunting pressure is to hike farther back into the timber than anyone else. Good advice, I suppose, if you happen to hunt where the habitat is publicly owned and extensive enough to allow you to put some distance between yourself and the bulk of the hunters. Sadly, such places are rare.

Most of us, though, will share public or private land with other hunters on opening day. So the choice is yours. You can whine

The best way to handle hunting pressure is to put your stand in a place where you can let other hunters push deer past your stand.

about the hunting pressure or you can accept the fact that hunting pressure is part of the game and make it work for you. I prefer the latter strategy.

There really is no big, dark secret to making hunting pressure work in your favor. It boils down to this: (1) Determine where the hunting pressure will be concentrated. (2) Determine where deer are most likely to go to escape the hunting pressure. (3) Select a stand along the route deer are most likely to use as they attempt to evade other hunters or take a stand in the escape cover itself. (4) Stay put long enough to let it happen.

DETERMINING WHERE HUNTING PRESSURE ORIGINATES

Sometimes this step is as simple as locating the parking lot of a public hunting area. Let's use as an example a 3,000-acre parcel of public land I have hunted on most opening days for the last 30 years. When I started hunting the property, there were no parking areas. Those of us who hunted simply pulled our vehicles over to the side of the gravel road. (In some places, this is still the rule and it is your job to determine where hunters park and walk in.) Over the years, three parking areas have been added and these areas account for the bulk of the access to the property. I also know from experience that a few hunters will walk in from a farm on the north side of the property and a few from a farm on the other side of the valley.

Since most hunters do not want to work any harder than they have to, the majority of the hunters will begin their morning hunt on stands within a quarter mile of these access points. As they get bored or cold, some will move to other stands deeper in the timber, some will attempt to still-hunt, and a few will gather with friends to conduct deer drives. All of this activity will move deer.

DETERMINING WHERE DEER WILL GO TO ESCAPE HUNTERS

With up-to-date aerial photographs, you can locate the places deer will be attracted to during periods of heavy hunting pressure without getting up from your kitchen table. Deer go to those places where they are least likely to be disturbed. This usually means thick cover.

One opening morning many years ago I received a valuable lesson in just how important thick cover is to a whitetail and how reluctant they are to leave the security of that cover, even in the face of heavy hunting pressure. Early in the morning I watched a doe and fawn slip into a thick patch of blowdowns and bramble directly across the narrow valley from where I was perched. Because there was snow on the ground, I could see them easily. All day I sat in my stand and all day those two deer stuck to that house-sized maze of branches and briar. Twice, hunters came and sat just above the thicket. One hunter still-hunted along the ridge and skirted just below the deer. Two different groups of hunters drove the sidehill, but in both instances the deer held their ground and the drivers went around, instead of through, that patch of forbidding cover. I've never forgotten the lesson that doe and her fawn taught me. When you are trying to determine where deer will go in the face of opening-day pressure, try to pinpoint the places hunters will be reluctant to go. The nasty bramble patch that doe and her fawn crawled into was a perfect example. So is a swamp where any hunter foolish enough to venture in is going to get wet feet. If it's nasty, wet, steep, deep, or just plain impossible to get at without the deer seeing, hearing, or smelling you, they will use it.

I would venture a guess that more big bucks are killed eluding one hunter and blundering into another than by any other method.

Speaking of places that deer go to escape hunting pressure; public land sometimes adjoins a game refuge on which no hunting is allowed. As you might expect, hunters tend to take stands along the boundary, hoping to get a shot at deer headed for the safety of the refuge. While some deer do seek the safety of the game refuge, the number of deer that live on the public land and use the game refuge is not nearly as high as most hunters assume. Most of the deer seek out cover within their own home areas and wait out the onslaught of hunters. Deer are homebodies. It takes intense pressure to force them to leave an area with which they are intimately familiar.

I should point out that in intensely agricultural areas of the country where whitetail habitat is limited to small woodlots and skinny creek bottoms—areas literally crawling with hunters on opening day—mature deer have learned that their best odds of surviving lie not in seeking out the few patches of heavy cover, cover that is almost sure to hold a hunter or two, but rather in getting smack dab in the middle of the biggest parcel of harvested cropland they can find. Since most of these regions are shotgun-only, the best hunters can do is watch the distant deer through binoculars and spotting scopes and drool. This kind of adaptation is what makes the whitetail deer such a challenging species to hunt.

CHOOSING AN OPENING-DAY STAND

You have two choices when it comes to selecting a stand for opening day. You can look for a stand somewhere along the escape route you think deer will use as they attempt to evade hunters and reach a safe area, or you can hunt from a stand within the escape cover itself. Most hunters choose option number one. Sitting in a stand overlooking an area you suspect deer will be traveling through as they try to evade other hunters will usually result in a number of deer sightings during the day. Everyone likes to see deer. Seeing deer keeps us from getting bored, keeps our spirits up. And there is no doubt that

47

Anytime hunting pressure is a major influence on deer movement, as it is on the opening weekend of the season in many states, your best option is to stay put on stand.

many a fine buck has hit the dirt while trying to slip along an escape trail, through a funnel, or across a saddle being watched by an alert, keen-eyed hunter.

Few hunters try option number two, which is hunting right in the thick stuff itself. There is good reason for this. The thick stuff is not fun to hunt. You can't see very far in the kind of cover a big buck looks for when the guns start going off, so you can forget about watching a parade of deer. Sitting a stand in the thick stuff and seeing nothing while guns are going off all around you will test your commitment. Most hunters who try to hunt in the heaviest cover give up after only an hour or two. I don't blame them. But I will tell you this, if it is the biggest buck in the neighborhood you want and if you want him bad enough, a stand in the meanest, nastiest, thickest, wettest, most gosh-awful stuff you can find is the place to be waiting when the fireworks start. Big bucks get to be big bucks by going places where nobody finds them once the guns start cracking.

HOW TO STAY PUT ON STAND

This is a tough one. The world we live in does not reward patience. Those who are energetic and hard-drivers seem to pull out ahead of the pack. So it is difficult to live in that kind of environment 51 weeks out of the year and then suddenly slam on the brakes and sit tight on a stand for eight hours a day for several days in a row. Most hunters just can't do it. Since deer hunting is supposed to be fun and not some kind of endurance test, let's look at a workable alternative to sitting in one stand all day. I call the alternative "musical stands," and it goes like this: Through scouting or using your experience from other years with the area you are hunting, pre-select three stand sites, one for the morning hours, one for midday, and a third for the evening hunt. Let's say that shooting hours begin at 7 A.M. and end at 5 P.M. You sit the morning stand from first light until late morning, say 11 A.M., at which time you hike to the midday stand and stay there until 2 or 3 P.M., when you hike to the pre-selected evening stand for the rest of the day. The key here is to have the stand sites pre-selected. If you do not, you will simply join the legions of hunters who spend hours each day wandering aimlessly around the woods looking for a good place to sit for a couple of hours. If you pre-select your stand sites, you will have confidence in each stand. Confidence breeds optimism, and optimism helps you stay alert and pay attention while on stand.

6

HUNTING RUB
LINES FROM ABOVE

I'll admit to being old enough to remember when buck rubs were still thought to be made by bucks attempting to rub the dead velvet off their antlers in late summer and early fall. We know today that this is not the case. Sure, a buck will sometimes help to expedite the process of shedding the velvet by a little judicious rubbing, but this activity accounts for only a tiny fraction of the rubs found in the woods. We now know that rubs serve as signposts in the whitetail's world. The gleaming inner layers of a rubbed sapling easily catch the eye of deer in the dark woods. Once visually attracted to the rub, the whitetail's keen sense of smell reads the message left behind by the buck that made the rub. As individually distinctive as our own fingerprints, the smells left behind, predominately from secretions from the buck's forehead gland, identify the buck to other deer. Those who study such things suspect that the rubs serve two main purposes. First, the rubs help establish a territory within which an individual buck is declaring his dominance over other bucks. Second, it is suspected that the olfactory signals left behind on rubs help to synchronize estrous cycles in the doe population. We do not know everything there is to know about buck rubs; hopefully, we never will. But know this. If you seek a mature buck early in the season when the weather is warm and scraping activity is still weeks away, then finding a rub line is your best connection to such an animal.

The first bucks to make rubs each September are the biggest, most dominant animals. You will not find a lot of rubs at this time. In fact, in most parts of the country, because mature bucks are in short supply, you will often have to look long and hard to find that first rub. Once you find it, though, it should lead you to another and another. This searching for rubs early in the fall can be a time-consuming ad-

Mature bucks are the first to begin rubbing in early fall. Locate a good rub line at this time and you have found the travel route of a dandy buck.

venture, but if you are serious about hunting for a mature buck at this time of the year the search will be time well spent. However, I must warn you that your search could prove fruitless. There are many areas of the country where a mature buck—a whitetail buck of at least three-and-a-half years—is a very rare critter. If you hunt such an area and fail to find rubs in early to mid-September, the fault lies not with you, but with a game management philosophy that does not encourage a balanced age structure in the deer herd. Simply put, no matter how hard you search, you can't find what ain't there.

If your hunting area is home to a mature buck, or even better a handful of such animals, then luck is on your side because it is during this time period (when a mature buck is beginning to make rubs) that his travel patterns are as predictable as they will ever be during the hunting season. In September, when the big boys are beginning to rub in most parts of the country, the bucks are not yet as inclined to roam far and wide in search of receptive does as they will be come late October and much of November. The bucks are still locked in that lazy, repetitious pattern of late summer/early fall, which basically revolves around two activities: eating and resting. (Reminds me of some teenagers in my own house.) Anyway, life is good and living is as easy as it gets for a whitetail at this time of the year.

When you find a rub line, odds are good that it will be located either along the route the buck uses to move between the primary food source and his bedding area or in the buck's staging area. Let's look at both possibilities.

As the amount of daylight in a 24-hour period begins to diminish in early fall, a buck's system begins to produce more testosterone, the hormone that in a few weeks will be surging through the buck's system in such quantity as to transform this secretive, shy critter into a bold, daring, sex-craved aggressor. But for now, the buck is just beginning to feel his oats, as the old saying goes. In an annual ritual as old as the species, the buck now begins to rub his antlers on saplings. Whether he is purposefully making the rubs to leave visual and scent communication for other deer or simply flexing and strengthening his neck and chest muscles for the deadly combat with other bucks just around the corner, as some speculate, is anyone's guess. Why the buck begins to make rubs is not nearly as important as the fact that make them he does, and those rubs are the best information you can have at your disposal when it comes to hanging a stand in a position from which to intercept the buck.

A mature buck is a creature of habit at this time of year. In late afternoon the buck will rise from his bed, stretch, relieve himself, and then begin the trek to his favorite feeding area. He is not in any hurry. If it is warm, odds are good he will stop for a drink at a pond or spring seep along the way. Chances are he will nip at a few leaves, crunch an acorn or two, and nip the tips of the tenderest plants he encounters. When he finds a suitable sapling, the buck will lower his head, engage the sapling with his antlers, and produce what we call a rub. The whole thing might take less than a minute, or he might spend 20 minutes playing out the ancient game. Big bucks are rarely in a hurry. Upon reaching the feeding area, if he feels comfortable strolling out into the field, meadow, or clearcut to feed, he will do so. Often the buck will not feel comfortable entering the opening, especially if it is not near dark. In this case, the buck will spend some time in what is commonly called a "staging area," basically just a place where the buck hangs out until it is dark enough for him to feel comfortable entering the opening. Because these staging areas see a lot of use during the period when mature bucks are beginning to make rubs, they are often littered with rubs.

Once the buck feels secure in the feeding area, he will emerge and feed. When full he will lie down and chew his cud for an hour or so before rising again to feed once more. He may wander over to the edge of the opening a few times during the evening to work over some unlucky sapling, which accounts for all the rubs you routinely find along the edges of major feeding areas. This pattern will be repeated until near first light, when the buck will slowly make his way back to the bedding area. Sometimes the buck will follow the same trail or general route that he used to move from his bedding area to the food source the previous evening, but often the return path is completely different.

Luckily for bowhunters, this pattern will hold true until about the last week of October unless the food source changes or the buck responds to hunting pressure and goes nocturnal.

A freshly rubbed sapling almost glows like a beacon in the woods on a gloomy day.

As I've indicated, finding these early season rubs is the real challenge. Once you locate some rubs, determining what the buck is up to when making them, which direction he is headed, when the best time to hunt the rubs is, and where to position your stand or stands is the fun part.

Following a rub line can be as easy as following the hash marks down the middle of a two-lane highway or more difficult than the greatest mystery the rumpled detective Columbo ever unraveled. Most rub lines fall somewhere in between, the difficulty factor being based upon the number of rubs, how close they are together, the terrain, and the habitat. For instance, all else being equal, a rub line is easier to follow on flat ground than in hilly country. I have not met anyone yet who can see through a mound of dirt or stone. Likewise, a rub line is usually easier to follow in relatively open hardwoods where you might be able to see 50 to 100 yards ahead than it is through some nasty thicket or swamp where visibility is measured in feet instead of yards. I say usually, however, as sometimes I have found rub lines much easier to follow in thick stuff than in open timber, simply because mature bucks tend to make more rubs in heavy cover than they do in open or semi-open timber.

Once I find a rub I scan in a complete circle looking for more rubs. Remember to look both near and far. It is easy to get so focused on trying to spot another rub out at the far edge of your vision range that a rub 30 feet away goes unnoticed. Sometimes it helps to drop down on your knees to get a perspective from a lower angle. Many times I have spotted rubs from my knees that I overlooked while standing up. If I don't see another rub I take my best guess as to which direction the buck was going when he made the rub and head in that direction. Sometimes this is easy, sometimes not. If the rub is along a trail, it is a good bet that the buck's next rub will be along that trail, as well. I follow the trail in one direction as far as I can, taking note of all rubs and other sign I find along the way. I then return to my starting point and take the trail in the other direction. This is the most common method of using rub lines to determine a buck's route between bedding cover and the prime feeding area. Usually, rubs will be most plentiful near the bedding area and again near the feeding area. If it is a fair distance between the bedding area and the feeding site, say a half-mile or so, it is not unusual for there to be stretches of 100 or more yards with no rubs along the mid-section of the trail.

When I follow a rub line to a bedding area, I try not to actually enter the bedding area itself. I don't have any proof that a mature buck will vacate a bedding area or change his habits just because you bust him in his bedroom a time or two, but I don't take the chance that he will. When the rub line leads me to what looks like a prime bedding area, usually either a high ridge or a nasty thicket, I back off and start looking for places to hang the stand.

Of course, before you hang a stand you will want to know if the buck is using the trail in the mornings, evenings, or both. By studying tracks in the trail and the rubs themselves this is easy to determine. If most of the tracks are headed from the bedding area to the food source, the trail is being used in the evening. If the tracks are mostly going the other direction, the trail is being used by the buck in the morning as he returns to his bed. And if big tracks are going both directions, the buck is probably using the same trail to exit and enter his bedding area.

If saplings are rubbed predominately on the side facing the bedding area, odds are the buck is making the rubs as he moves from the bedding area to the food source. If the rubs are mostly on the side facing the feeding area, they are most likely morning rubs. And if you find rubs that show wear and tear on all sides, along with tracks on the trail pointing in both directions, you have solid confirmation that a buck is using the same trail for morning and evening.

I usually follow a rub line twice. The first time I am concentrating hard on finding the next rub, and I have learned from experience that when I am focused on looking for rubs, I often overlook other important information. The second time I walk a rub line my eyes are open for deer sign I might have missed on my first pass or maybe terrain features that I failed to notice. A little tuft of hair caught on barbed wire, for instance, might just lead to the perfect stand location along the rub line. Sometimes I am amazed at the obvious clues I miss when trying to put together the pieces of a rub line on the first pass. On the second pass I am still searching for additional sign, but I am also looking for the place where I will hang my stand.

Several times I have seen fenceposts rubbed right in two and once, on a farm I hunt in western Illinois, I saw a telephone pole that had been so severely rubbed it had to be replaced. The resident bucks began rubbing the new telephone pole as soon as it was installed.

Most of the time I will end up hanging it somewhere close to the bedding area. The trick here is to have the stand positioned close enough to the buck's bedding area so that you can catch him exiting in the evening while shooting light remains. Because mature bucks are often in their bedding area before most other deer in the morning, a stand located there also gives you the greatest leeway for catching the buck during that pink time before dawn when most big bucks make their way back. But there is a fine balancing act; put the stand too close to where the buck beds and you risk spooking him when you approach and climb into the stand for the evening hunt. If the stand is too near the bedding area and you do not take the buck as he enters, you might spook him when exiting the stand after the morning hunt. How close is too close depends upon a lot of different circumstances. The size of the bedding area is a major consideration. If the bedding area is large, say a big swamp, a large cutover that has grown up dog-hair thick, or an extensive ridge where the buck might bed down anywhere along its length, I'll often snug my stand right up tight to the bedding area and take my chances that the buck is bedding deep enough within the cover that I will go undetected. If the bedding area is small, I may put my stand several hundred yards away along the rub line just to make sure that I do not bust the buck in his bedroom.

Terrain has a lot to do with how close I approach the bedding area, as well. In hill country, bucks almost always bed up high, sometimes right on top of the ridges, but more often on little spines that jut off the main ridge. Either way, they have the elevation advantage, and when a buck holds the high ground it is very difficult to approach without alerting him. When hunting hill country I will often place my stand well down the ridge, or maybe even down in the flats, so as not to disturb the area where the buck is bedding. However, when it comes to ridges, I break my rule of not disturbing the bedding area and actually follow the rub line right to the ridge itself. I do this because very often a buck will have a rub line established along the trail it uses to move from high ground to the valley in the evening and back again to the ridge in the morning and will also have one that runs along the ridge itself. Rub lines that parallel a ridge are dynamite stand locations.

One reason is that bucks spend more time during the day up on the ridges than they do down low. In hill country, if you are going to catch a buck on his feet during that first or last hour of daylight, odds are good it is going to be from a stand on a ridge.

Another reason I really get pumped when I find a rub line along a ridge is that I know that even if I do not kill that buck during the early part of the bow season, there is a good chance I will get a crack at him later in the season when bucks begin serious scraping and snooping for does. It is very common for a scrape line to appear along rub lines, and nowhere is this more common than along a ridgeline string of rubs. Even after bucks pretty much abandon the rubs and scrapes and go into that single-minded search mode for does in days prior to the first wave of does entering estrous, you could do worse than to hunt along a ridge littered with rubs. Bucks know that in hilly terrain the does tend to bed high, as well, and this is where the bucks will be cruising during all hours of the day.

7

SETTING UP ON SCRAPES

I've sat in treestands from which I could peer down on scrapes from the godforsaken, thorny scrub brush of south Texas to the dark spruce forests of northern Alberta and 20 or so states and provinces in between, and I'm happy to report that the sight of a big, fresh scrape still makes my heart do funny things. I'm not sure why this is true, because I have not killed all that many big bucks while hunting over scrapes. In fact, to be perfectly blunt, I think that scrape hunting has been blown all out of proportion. Because of all the hype, many hunters today figure the hunt is as good as over when they find a string of good scrapes. Sometimes it is. But I can tell you from my own painful experiences that if you put all of your faith in hunting over scrapes, you are going to be disappointed a lot more often than you are going to be elated.

Does this mean that hunting over scrapes is a waste of time and effort? It does not. It simply means that if you are going to spend your valuable hours in the woods hunting over scrapes you had better make darn sure that you are hunting over the right scrapes at the right time and that you are set up properly to take full advantage of the opportunity when a buck comes back for a visit.

Don't worry, I'm not going to try to dazzle you with a bunch of scientific research. Although I rely heavily on this ongoing research for my own use, this is a hunting book, not a scientific journal, so we will take an in-depth look at scrapes from a hunter's perspective.

The overhanging branch is the main communication center at any scrape, and bucks will go to great lengths to deposit scent on it.

The questions I am most often asked about scrapes at seminars or in deer camps around the country are these:

Why do bucks make scrapes? In the whitetail's world a scrape has two purposes. A buck uses a scrape to identify himself to other bucks. In this role, the scrape is a buck's way of declaring his dominance. But since all deer are attracted to scrapes, a scrape can also serve as an advertisement for willing does. This advertisement of the buck's scent is left behind in both the scrape itself and the overhanging branch and relays a lot of information to the doe concerning the buck's social status in the local deer herd.

How important is that overhanging branch? The overhanging branch is all-important. During 40-some years of tromping around in the places whitetail deer call home, I have never seen an active scrape that did not include an overhanging branch. On occasion you will find a small scrape in a field or meadow a good distance from any tree, but these are simply spots that a buck has pawed out of sexual frustration and excitement, usually right after a doe has urinated in that spot.

Many scrapes originate because of an overhanging branch. A buck will work his antlers in an overhanging branch, rub his face and forehead on the branch, and often chew and lick the branch. While doing all of this the buck is depositing scent from his forehead glands, nasal glands, pre-orbital glands, and from his saliva. All of this scent serves to identify an individual. One buck can identify another buck by the scent left behind on an overhanging branch.

Overhead branches are worked by bucks all year long. Many hunters refer to these branches as "licking branches," a term I prefer to use when referring to branches that do not develop into scrapes. Some licking branches are used for many years and visited by numerous bucks, but for some reason they just never develop into scrapes. A well-used licking branch is an excellent location for a stand because, unlike a scrape that is only going to be active for a few days or weeks each year, a licking branch is likely to get attention on any given day during the season. The most bucks I have ever personally seen work a licking branch in a single day was six, but with surveillance cameras it is not unusual to record a dozen visits to a licking stick in a 24-hour period.

Licking sticks are not easy to locate, but they are worth the effort to find. Most will be found hanging over deer trails about five feet off the ground, although I have seen two licking sticks that bucks had to stand up on their hind legs to reach. I suspect that these started off as licking sticks at a normal height and with years of use had been broken and worn away until the bucks were forced to stand to reach them. Sometimes you get lucky and the tip of the licking branch will resemble a pencil or wooden dowel, with no new growth on the last six or eight inches, a result of constant rubbing and nibbling by visiting bucks. More often you will have to rely upon locating overhanging branches through less obvious clues. I've actually found more licking branches by observing deer working them than I have while looking for them. But enough about licking branches; let's get back to the overhanging branch with a scrape beneath it.

I'm convinced that the overhead branch is the main communication center at any scrape. I've watched countless bucks (and some does) come into scrapes and totally ignore the scrape itself or perhaps give the dirt a cursory sniff and then turn all of their attention to the overhanging branch. Sometimes deer will spend several minutes nuzzling, licking, and rubbing an overhead branch. On many occasions I have had the same buck visit a scrape two or three times during a day and on each visit go directly to the overhanging branch.

When do bucks make most of the scrapes? In regions with a short, intense, concentrated rut, the vast majority of scrapes are made during the two to three weeks preceding peak breeding. This is when the majority of the scrapes are pawed out, but some scraping activity begins in late summer and continues well into winter.

How often is a scrape revisited? This depends upon the scrape. Some scrapes are never revisited, others are only visited haphazardly, and still others, the ones of most importance to us, are checked daily and sometimes more than once during a 24-hour period.

How many bucks will visit a single scrape? It depends on the location of the scrape and how many bucks are in the area. A scrape that is not in a high traffic area is not going to get much attention, no matter how many bucks call the surrounding habitat home. But a scrape located near the junction of several major trails, on a heavily used crossing, or at the main entrance to a prime feeding area is likely to become a major attraction with bucks in the area. For years, I thought that it would be the maximum if a half-dozen different bucks visited an individual scrape. I was wrong. When friends and I began using surveillance cameras to record the activity on scrapes, we quickly found that an astonishing number of different bucks will visit the same scrape. The record for our group is held by Tom Indrebo who in a single evening recorded 21 different bucks visiting a single scrape on his farm in western Wisconsin.

Where is the best place to look for scrapes? Scrapes are most numerous along edges and on trails. This is because deer spend a lot of time in these areas and because a scrape is an advertisement. Just as McDonalds will spend its advertising dollars on a billboard along the busiest interstate, bucks like to paw out scrapes in places where they are going to get some business, too. As we will discuss shortly, however, the most obvious and visible scrapes are not always the best ones to hunt over.

What is a scrape line? A scrape line is nothing more than a number of scrapes made by the same buck as he moves through his home area. A scrape line is most likely to be located between the buck's bedding area and the main food source or between doe family groups which the buck will check on with increasing frequency as the time for does to be entering estrous nears. Scrape lines will

Many scrapes, like this one, are not easy to see and unless you train yourself to really look for them, you will walk past a lot of them.

Once you see one, you will always recognize a freshly worked scrape like this one.

often appear along rub lines, which are usually, but not always, made prior to scrapes.

A scrape line along a field edge or down an old logging road is easy to follow; one that meanders through the timber takes a bit more detective work to unravel. Sometimes a buck will paw out a couple dozen scrapes in a single night of carousing and a scrape line will appear literally overnight, but more commonly a scrape line develops over several days or a week. Each time the buck travels the route he paws out another scrape or two and the end result is a scrape line.

What is a cluster scrape or a community scrape? As the name suggests, a cluster scrape occurs when a group of scrapes are made very close together. Often the edge of one scrape will be touching the other. I've seen many that resemble four- or five-leaf clovers. The individual scrapes within a cluster are made by individual bucks, all trying to let the other bucks know that they are bad to the bone. Usually, these cluster scrapes will eventually be transformed into one big, community scrape. Most of the community scrapes I've seen were about the size of a bathtub or kitchen table, and a few were much larger. You could have parked an F-150 pickup truck in the largest community scrape I've ever seen.

How do I know which scrapes to hunt over? I wish I had an infallible answer for you, but I do not. The best I can do is give you some tips on how to separate the low percentage scrapes from the high percentage ones.

- A lone scrape is never as appealing as a scrape that is part of a scrape line.
- Community scrapes are high percentage scrapes simply because there are so many bucks visiting them. However, research has proven what most of us who hunt scrapes have known for a long time, namely, that 75 to 90 percent of all visits to scrapes occur at night. Your odds are no better at a

community scrape and might be worse because most tend to be located in semi-open areas, often along the edges of fields or clearcuts, places where daytime scrape visits are very rare. Researchers have also discovered that bucks that do visit scrapes during shooting light are mostly young bucks. The old-timers are so nocturnal that they rarely show up at a scrape during shooting hours.

- Many scrapes never get revisited. If the dirt in a scrape is crusted over or full of leaves and twigs, that scrape is not being hit and you are wasting your time hunting over it.

- The very best scrapes to hunt over are precisely those that most hunters either never find or avoid when they do find. I'm talking about scrapes in thick cover or on the edge of bedding cover. The reason these scrapes are your best bet for taking a mature buck is because these are the scrapes most likely to be visited at dawn, dusk, and perhaps at midday.

- As the breeding period of the rut approaches, scrapes show up everywhere, with every buck in the woods getting in on the action. But early in the scraping period, the scrapes you find will be made by the dominant buck or bucks in the area. These are the ones you want to concentrate on.

- Once a number of does are in heat, hunting over scrapes is a waste of time. A little buck may still visit a scrape hoping to get lucky, but the mature bucks are either with does or trailing does during this period. There are better places to hunt at this time.

- When the rut is on the downhill slide, with most of the does having already been bred, take some time to check out a few of the major scrapes. If you find one that is being worked, hang a stand and sit tight. When a hot doe becomes tough to find, the big boys will go back to visiting their most productive scrapes.

Is there anything I can do to encourage bucks to visit the scrape I am hunting? Absolutely! I never just sit on a scrape and hope the buck that made it or one of his buddies will show up on their own. I spend a lot of time rattling and calling when hunting over scrapes. When a big buck laid up in heavy cover for the day hears a buck grunting and a doe bleating down by one of his scrapes, what do you suppose goes through his mind? Ditto for rattling. Don't just sit there, make something happen.

If I'm hunting in fairly open timber I will use a decoy, as well. A decoy gives that buck the confirmation he is seeking. He heard a deer, now he sees a deer. The deal is completed. Also, many of the biggest bucks will often either scent check a scrape from some distance downwind or visually inspect a scrape from a distance to see if there are any deer hanging around. A decoy provides them with what they expect to see.

Scent is another big plus. The last big buck I killed over a scrape provides the perfect example of the role scent can play in scrape hunting.

In the gathering gloom of a late November evening, the big buck heard the sound of clashing antlers reverberating through the river bottoms. Although the distinctive clatter of bone-on-bone was over 300 yards away, the buck instantly pinpointed the source of the sound, spun on big, blunt-toed hooves, and beelined towards the sound. I heard his hooves pounding the hard, sun-baked Kansas clay. I let the rattling bag drop to my side on its lanyard and plucked the Mathews off the bow hook. The buck jumped a sagging, barbed-wire fence 30 yards away and straight downwind of where I perched 20 feet up a gnarly, wind-tortured cottonwood. When he skidded to a sudden halt behind a thick stand of scrub willow, I figured that despite all of my precautions to control my human odor, the old buck had picked up just a whiff of scent and was now letting his brain determine whether the dreaded scent was near enough or fresh enough to be of concern. It seemed like forever, although it was probably only 30 seconds, before the buck's brain gave him the "no problem" answer I was hoping it would deliver. The buck curled around the point of the willow patch and went directly to a scrape I had "tuned up" hours earlier. The buck's antlers were hooking the overhanging willow branch when my broadhead sliced silently through both of his lungs.

That buck happens to be the most recent buck I've taken over a tuned-up scrape, but he darn sure was not the first and he won't be the last. I'm a big fan of tuning up scrapes, but despite the success I've enjoyed hunting over them, I won't try to convince you that all you have to do to see more bucks and bigger bucks is to pour some pee in a scrape and get ready for a buck parade. It does not work that way. I've carefully scented a lot of scrapes and then hunted over them without ever seeing a buck. So why bother? Because over the past 20 years I have had more bucks visit scrapes that I have tuned up with scent than those not tuned up.

I believe the biggest advantage you gain from adding scent to scrapes and overhanging branches is that the scent you add triggers a response from any buck visiting the scrape. Perhaps that response is one of aggression or dominance if buck urine or tarsal gland scent is used. It may trigger sexual frustration if doe-in-estrous urine is employed. Or maybe all scents simply trigger the natural curiosity of the whitetail. This would certainly help explain why researchers have found bucks to sometimes be attracted to scrapes that have been tainted with human urine or even those sickeningly sweet smelling sprays designed to keep the interior of your car smelling like brand new. The bottom line is that I don't care what is going through the buck's mind. All I care about is doing everything in my power to make sure that if a buck is going to visit a scrape during shooting hours, the scrape he selects is the one I'm sitting over. If you can make a buck remember that he smelled something good in a certain scrape you are on your way to accomplishing that goal.

Hunting over scrapes is not a high percentage tactic, but nice bucks are killed over scrape lines each season.

HOW TO TUNE UP A SCRAPE

When I first began messing around with deer scents, and later adding scents to scrapes, deciding what scent to use was easy. All we had was what we called "doe pee." Today, there are over 100 choices on the market. Scents based on deer urine are still the biggest sellers, but many have now added tarsal gland, interdigital gland, and even forehead gland to the mix. Synthetics are big too, as are the so-called "solid scents," the pastes, gels, crystals, and pellets. I have not used all of the different scents available today, but I have tested a lot of them, and although I have had better results with some than others, I would not conclude that my in-the-field tests really prove much. If a buck happens to visit a scrape I've tuned up with product A on Monday, but I don't see a buck while hunting over a scrape juiced up with product B on Tuesday, does it mean that product A is more attractive to bucks than product B? Probably not. Instead, I pick my "favorites" using different criteria. How long does a buck hang around when he visits one of my tuned-up scrapes? If a buck spends a lot of time sniffing and licking at the scrape and overhanging branch, then I figure whatever scent I used has really gotten his attention. I've had bucks spend over ten minutes at scrapes I've scented. One Illinois buck came back to visit a scrape I was sitting over six times in one day. You can bet that the scent I was using in that scrape is on my all-time-favorites list.

More important than what brand of scent you leave behind at the scrape is the brand of scent you do not leave behind. I'm talking about human odor, of course. When I tune up a scrape I wear a Scent-Lok suit, rubber boots (often hip boots), and rubber gloves. A mature buck lives by his nose and if his nose tells him that a human has been at his scrape, I don't care what brand of scent you use, odds are good that buck will not visit that scrape again.

To tune up a scrape I begin by using a stick or a garden trowel to work up the soil in the scrape. I usually work in some gel or paste lure at the same time. If it is a scrape that I know I might not be able to hunt for several days, I bury an H.S. Buc-n-Rut Scent Wafer an inch under the soil or I take a small jar or 35mm film canister, add scent, poke some holes in the lid, and bury it an inch or so under the surface.

Next, I pour a large handful of Magic Scrape into the center of the scrape. Magic Scrape is a specially blended, waterproof soil that bucks find very attractive by itself, but I spice it up a little by making a depression in the mound of Magic Scrape and adding a half-ounce of liquid scent. That's it for the scrape; now on to the really important stuff, the overhanging branch.

Every scrape worth hunting over has an overhanging branch and it is here that the real scent communication between deer takes place. Many times I have watched deer come into a scrape and never even bother to sniff the scrape itself but spend minutes licking, chewing, rubbing their faces on, and hooking the overhanging branch with their antlers. A buck leaves scent behind from his tarsal, salivary, forehead, nasal, and preorbital glands as well as his urine when he works an overhanging branch. Add a little of your favorite scent to the branch itself and then take a scent wick and secure it to the branch with wire or a plastic tie. Don't be cheap when it comes to applying scent to that scent wick. Soak it until it won't hold any more.

NOT ALL SCRAPES ARE CREATED EQUAL

When I first began hunting over scrapes I only had one prerequisite in choosing the scrape. Size. The bigger the better, I figured. The problem with really big scrapes, or community scrapes as they are commonly called because they are nearly always the work of more than one buck, is that they are usually found on the edge of a major feeding location, which in most whitetail habitats means a field. Does gather here each night to feed. Bucks come to sniff the does. One buck walks over and paws out a scrape. As soon as he walks off another steps up to the plate and then the next and the next and the next. The problem with these big scrapes is that nearly all of the action takes place at night. On rare occasions, when the testosterone is peaking in a mature buck's system, that buck may become so bold as to visit during shooting hours, but I'm not willing to bet my season on those odds. Instead, I look for scrapes in or near heavy cover, the kind of places a big buck is going to lay up in for part of the day. I want the scrape I tune up to be accessible to that buck. A scrape in such a location gives me an excellent chance of intercepting the buck as he enters his bedding area in early morning or as he exits in late afternoon. A tuned-up scrape in heavy cover is also one of my favorite places to pull an all-day sit, something I do quite often during the rut. Most deer get up out of their beds at midday to relieve themselves, stretch, and browse a little. Big bucks are no exception. Many times, when the scraping phase of the rut is in full swing, a buck will check a nearby scrape or two during this midday activity period.

TIMING YOUR TUNE UP

You will often read that the peak scraping period of the rut occurs during the two weeks prior to the first does entering estrous, and this information is accurate. During this two-week-long stretch every buck in the timber gets into the scraping mode. The problem with this period is that if you are hunting an area with a decent buck population, there are too many scrapes. With so many scrapes it is more difficult to elicit interest in your tuned-up scrape. Also, when scraping is at its peak it is nearly impossible to concentrate your efforts on a mature

When big buck specialist Randy Grawe works up a scrape he uses a stout stick in each fist and really tears up the soil.

buck. That is why my favorite time to tune up scrapes is before the peak of the scraping phase of the rut. Mature bucks begin scraping earlier, often as much as two weeks earlier than immature bucks.

I stick with adding scent to scrapes and hunting over scrapes right up until the bucks start chasing does. Once that action starts there are better places to hunt, but until then a tuned-up scrape can really tune up your season.

THE SCOOP ON MOCK SCRAPES

Mock scrapes were all the rage with bowhunters for a few years, but you don't hear much about them anymore. In fact, a whole generation of new bowhunters has come along since the mock scrape craze petered out. Many of these newcomers to the sport have never tried mock scraping, some have never even heard of it. That's too bad, because fake scrapes are one of the best tools the bowhunter has at his disposal for putting bucks right where he wants them.

Of course, there is a reason why you don't hear much about mock scrapes anymore. When mock scraping was big news in the bowhunting world, every hunter with a quiver full of arrows was running around the woods laying down fake scrapes. Many of these mock scrapes were made at the wrong time of the season or placed in bad locations. Either error means no visits. Some mock scrapes were contaminated with human scent, a big no-no when setting a fake scrape trap for Mr. Big. Others had no holding power. Some hunters think all you have to do is scrape away the leaves, pour in a little scent, and presto, every buck in the woods starts tearing it up. But mock scrapes rarely work that way. Many hunters decided that mock scrapes were just the product of some outdoor writer's imagination working overtime. It wasn't long before you did not read about mock scrapes in the magazines anymore.

Even though mock scrapes may have fallen on hard times with the rank-and-file, a few tight-lipped hunters have gone right on using and perfecting fake scrapes for putting big bucks right where they want them season after season. These hunters know that when a fake scrape is made the right way, at the right time, and in the right place, they can count on plenty of action. I cannot say with certainty that a properly presented mock scrape has never spooked a deer, but I can say with certainty that none of the dozens of deer—mostly bucks, but a few does and fawns as well—that I have watched visit mock scrapes have ever displayed anything but interest. Have I ever had deer ignore my mock scrapes? You bet I have. I've seen them step right in the fake scrape and never give it a second glance. But this kind of behavior has been rare. From what I have seen, I have to believe that most of the time, after a buck initially discovers a mock scrape, that buck will pay repeated visits. The most visits I've ever had from a single buck in one day is six, but many times I've had the same buck return two or three times during the day. Odds are good that if the buck is visiting that often during the day, he is doubling or tripling that output at night, when most scraping and scrape visitations are conducted.

I'm not sure what triggers a buck to make repeated visits to a fake scrape. It may be the dominance factor at work. Mature bucks may be especially anxious to meet this stranger who is bold enough to paw out scrapes within his home area. I think sex appeal certainly has something to do with it. When a buck's nose tells him that a hot-to-trot doe has been in the neighborhood, he does not forget her address. I'm sure that part of the appeal of a fake scrape is simply the whitetail's curiosity. But it's really not important to me whether it is one of these factors or a combination of all three that brings bucks back for repeat visits. The important thing is that bucks will return to visit a properly prepared, well-positioned mock scrape.

There are three important factors to take into consideration when making fake scrapes: timing, location, and preparation.

TIMING

Fake scrapes are not a peak-of-the-rut tactic as so many hunters assume. Instead, fake scrapes are at their best during pre-rut and the early stages of the rut. The biggest mistake I see hunters making when it comes to mock scrapes is making the fake scrapes too late in the season. If you wait until every buck in the woods is pawing out his string of scrapes, your scrapes are often lost among dozens or hundreds of others. My favorite time to make them is in September and early October, but I've made them as early as the 4th of July. Remember, you can't make them too early, but you can darn sure be too late.

Whenever possible I like to have my mock scrapes in position even before the big boy gets started. I have a hunch that a mature buck does not much care for the idea that another buck is scraping within his turf. Odds are good that the buck will visit these scrapes often in an attempt to identify the interloper.

I can tell you from experience that mock scrapes in place early have a much better chance of attracting a mature buck than a mock scrape that is not established until after the bucks have begun scraping themselves.

LOCATION

When you are looking for places to make mock scrapes remember that the easier you make it for deer to find your handiwork, the more action you will have. Open fields are no good because there are no overhanging branches. Thick cover has plenty of overhanging branches, but there is a good chance that a fake scrape in heavy cover will never be discovered. Edges and open stands of timber are the two prime locations for mock scrapes. Whitetail deer are fond of edge cover. They spend a lot of time feeding and moving along the seam where one type of vegetation meets another. When the scraping period of the rut begins, you will almost always find scrapes along a good edge. Ditto for semi-open timber. Think back to the places where you have found scrapes in the woods you hunt, maybe along that ridgeline or down that old logging road. Keep these places in mind when thinking location for mock scrapes. My very best action has always come high rather than low. Sure, you find a lot of scrapes in low places, but most of these are nighttime scrapes. Bucks tend to bed high. Mock scrapes on high ground are more likely to be visited by a big buck before he turns in for the morning or first thing in the evening when he gets out of his bed. Don't go into the bedding area, but get as close as you can.

PREPARING THE FAKE SCRAPE

I've been making fake scrapes for at least 20 years and each year I have refined my preparations. When I started out I simply found what looked like a good spot, took my boot and scraped away the leaves, dumped a little doe pee in the dirt, and called it good. As you might suspect, my reward was a lot of hours spent sitting over fake scrapes that attracted few deer. In fact, that first season I used fake scrapes, my journals remind me that only two deer visited my hastily created imitations. One was a button buck, the most curious of all of the deer in the woods, and the other was a basket-racked six point that I managed to miss at twelve yards as he stood with his face in the overhanging branch. That one encounter was enough to hook me, and I've been a fan of fake scrapes ever since.

Before I get into how I now prepare my mock scrapes, I want to emphasize two points that are vital. One is that the overhanging branch is more important than the scrape itself, and the other is that multiple fake scrapes (call it a fake scrape line) are more effective than a single mock scrape.

My main emphasis on any mock scrape is the overhanging branch. If there is not a suitable overhanging branch near where I want to make a mock scrape, I cut a branch from another tree and wire it to an existing branch or tree trunk so that it hangs about five feet above where I will put the mock scrape. As I stated earlier, I'm convinced that the overhanging branch, not the scrape itself, is the main communication center at any scrape.

When I began making mock scrapes I usually made just one. I enjoyed some success, but nothing great. Then I got to thinking that when hunting over real scrapes, I rarely did so over a lone scrape. So I began making fake scrape lines and business picked up dramatically. I'll usually put five to ten fake scrapes in a line, which takes more effort than making a single fake scrape, but my results have proven that the time and effort is well spent. Sometimes, if the terrain and habitat are suitable, I'll make two fake scrape lines, maybe one running along the edge where a thick stand of conifers abut hardwoods and the other along an abandoned logging road that dissects the edge. Then I'll put my stand overlooking the area where the two fake scrape lines cross (see illustration).

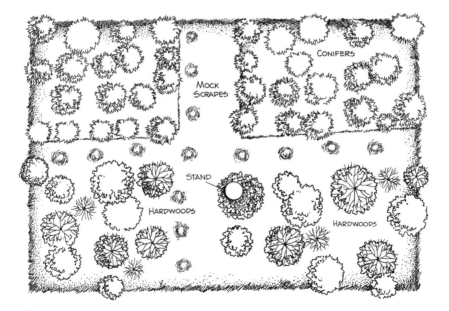

Before I get into how I make my mock scrapes, let me clarify something. I'll give you the brand names of the scents I use to make my mock scrapes, but I am not implying that these are the only scents that will do the job. There are a lot of good deer scents on the market today and some may do an even better job than the ones I use—but I know these work.

To summarize, then, these are the steps I use when making a mock scrape:

1. Find a live branch hanging four to five feet off the ground where you want to make a mock scrape. If a branch is not available, cut one and wire it to a tree so that the lower branches droop about five feet off the ground. Wire a scent wick to the branch and apply a scent containing forehead gland to the wick and the branch.

2. Beneath the branch use a garden trowel to clear all of the grass and leaves from a spot about the size of a beach ball. I like to use the trowel to work the soil up until it is soft enough to bury a Buc-n-Rut Scent Wafer an inch or two under the surface. This will keep bucks coming back for a long time. Before I began using the scent wafers, I used a small jar or 35mm film canister with urine-soaked cotton inside and holes poked in the lid so the odor could ooze out.

3. In the center of the scrape you have created, pour about a cupful of Primetime Magic Scrape. This is a waterproof, scent-impregnated soil that bucks find very appealing. In the center of the Magic Scrape, make a depression with the handle of the garden trowel and fill it with your favorite scent.

Using this method, you will have mock scrapes that keep on working for you between hunts, which is vitally important to success over mock scrapes.

8

HUNTING THE CHASE PHASE OF THE RUT

Back in my high school days I played a little third base. There was a skinny kid from one of the neighboring schools who gave me fits. The kid batted right-handed and was a straight pull hitter. This kid had never hit a ball to right field in his life. He would step up to the plate, dig in, wave the lumber, and then cock his head a bit to stare at me over his left shoulder. If I shifted towards the bag, he would slap one through the gap. If I covered that hole, he would lace one right over the bag. Every time we played that team, that kid made me look bad.

I got to thinking about those old high school games after an exciting, but frustrating day of bowhunting in northeast Iowa. It was the second week of November, the tenth to be precise. The morning was one of those you dream about. Clear, cold, and so calm you could hear a field mouse expel gas at a hundred yards. It was one of those mornings when you can just feel it. Something good was going to happen on this day.

Twice in the 20 minutes it took for shooting light to penetrate the night sky I heard deer running in the timber below the ridge on which I was perched. It was so still that the deer sounded like they were right under the oak to which I had strapped my stand, but they were probably far below along the little creek. The light was still murky when I heard another deer coming my way. The doe blasted from the edge of the woods, darted into a field of CRP, and came full tilt right at my tree along the seam where frost-coated grass met dark timber. Right behind her came a hog-fat, heavy-horned, wide-assed Iowa mega-buck. The doe blew right past my tree in an instant, the buck chugging along 20 yards behind. I drew and grunted at the buck with my mouth to get him to stop. If he heard me, he sure didn't acknowledge it. I let out a loud *blaaat!* He kept right on motoring. Flustered now, I swung with him, hit the release, and watched the yellow and white fletching disappear into the grass six feet behind him.

I was still kicking myself for taking a shot I shouldn't have when another doe came running over a gentle hill in the CRP field. Behind her were a pair of immature bucks, both basket-racked eight points. The trio darted into a finger of brush jutting into the CRP about 200 yards south of my perch and disappeared. The next hour was quiet. Then I heard deer running again, this time behind me. It was another doe being chased by a buck. They ran by below my stand in the heavy timber and then came squirting out that same finger of brush the threesome had run into an hour earlier. Through binoculars I studied the buck as he hot-footed after the doe across the CRP. It was a nice buck with long tines, but lacking the mass of a mature animal. I started to think about moving my stand to that brushy draw. An hour later, having seen no more deer, I did just that. I planned to hunt all day, might as well be in the best spot, right? Right! Guess where the next deer I saw walked? Yup, right under that oak I had just vacated. A nice one too and walking, not running. By

When the chase phase is on plan on, hunting all day whenever possible. You never know when bucks like these are going to come cruising past your stand.

dark I had seen three more bucks, although I think two of them were the same eight points I had seen cross the CRP earlier. One of them ran a doe in circles around that oak in which I had spent most of the morning. Kind of reminded me of how I felt when that skinny kid kept slapping balls through the holes where I used to be.

That's the chase phase for you. Lots of action, but trying to pick the precise stand location to best take advantage of that activity will drive you nuts.

WHAT IS THE CHASE PHASE?

The rut can be broken down into three phases: the scraping phase, the chase phase, and peak rut, which is when most of the actual breeding is accomplished. In the northern half of the whitetail's range, these three phases are often well defined because the breeding period occurs at a predictable time each year and is short and intense in duration. This is nature's way of insuring that the fawns will be dropped late enough in the spring to miss those deadly spring blizzards, but not so late that the youngsters are too small to make it through their first winter. In the southern states, where it is not critical that does give birth during a short and specific period, the breeding tends to drag out over weeks or even months, making it impossible to predict the timing of the main periods of the rut, much less the chase phase.

In those areas with a well-defined rut, the chase phase occurs at the tag end of the scraping period and just prior to the first wave of does entering estrous. The bucks have worked themselves into a frenzy by this time. They are primed and ready for action. To insure that they have a buck already on the hook when ready to be bred, does begin to give off scent signals a day or two prior to actually entering estrous. These signals are picked up by the bucks and the chase is on. The doe is not ready to stand for the buck yet, so she has to stay on the move constantly. When you get multiple does in this condition in your hunting area, you are in for a real circus. When it comes to seeing numbers of deer, both bucks and does, no other time compares with the short, but intense chase phase of the rut.

Because the chase phase is short-lived, timing is critical. Fortunately, predicting when the chase phase will occur is not difficult. The peak of the breeding period, a week- to ten-day-long whitetail orgy during which about 70 percent of the does are bred, falls roughly on about the same dates annually. The moon phase, the weather, herd condition, and hunting pressure can all have an influence on the exact timing and the intensity of daytime movement during the breeding period, but the dates will not vary by more than a few days in either direction from year to year. Nearly all game and fish departments will be able to furnish you with the dates of the peak of the breeding period in the state you are hunting. Once you know that the peak of the breeding period is from, let's say, November 15 to 25 in the state you are hunting, you can bet that the chase phase is going to occur sometime in the week prior to the beginning of the peak of breeding. In this case, I would be looking for chase phase action between November 8 and 15. Don't expect the chase phase to last the entire eight days; a couple of days of non-stop chasing is more the norm. The exact timing will depend upon the dates of the peak of breeding for that year.

The chase phase is one of my favorite times to be in the woods. If you are in decent whitetail country, seeing deer is almost a sure

Rattling, calling, decoying, and using scents are all very effective during the chase phase.

thing. However, seeing deer is the easy part. Setting up so that one of those bucks saunters by your stand within bow range is the frustrating part. Whitetail deer are unpredictable critters most of the time anyway, but when you've got a bunch of sex-crazed bucks chasing unwilling, frightened does around, the unpredictability factor skyrockets. I don't have any sure cures, but here are some of the things that have worked for me:

- Use a doe decoy. I do a lot of hunting over decoys and I usually prefer a buck decoy, but during the chase phase, because bucks tend to rush up to every doe they see, I've found that a doe decoy draws more attention. The very best set-up is a buck and a doe decoy. During the chase phase a buck cannot stand it if he thinks another buck already has a doe. Whether you use a single doe or a buck and doe, be sure the decoy is easily visible. Field edges, clearcuts, logging roads, natural woodland openings, and tree-studded pastures are all good bets. The more directions from which a buck can spot the decoy and the greater the distance, the more bucks your decoy attracts.

- Use a good doe-in-estrous urine. Don't put it right on the decoy, though. If you do, the odor will get on your clothing when you handle the decoy and you don't want to be smelling like a doe in heat and drawing attention to yourself. I like to jab a stick in the ground at the rear of the decoy and place a cotton ball or scent wick saturated with scent on a stick. Some guys just pour the scent on the ground, but I think the cotton ball or wick holds the scent longer. You don't need the urine to attract the buck to the decoy, but it will hold the buck's attention for a long time and allow you to get the perfect angle for the shot.

- Hunt funnels. That's worn advice, but it is still valid. A buck may wander through the funnel in his search for does or a harassed doe may pull a buck through the funnel behind her. Either way, you are a winner.

- Hunt food sources in the evening. If you know where the does are doing most of their feeding, that is the place to be in late afternoon when the chase phase is in progress. The bucks know these places too, and although they care little about eating, they will cruise through these whitetail cafeterias hoping to catch a doe or two chowing down. Great places for a decoy, too.

- Do a lot of calling and rattling. This is prime time to grunt in or rattle up a buck. The bucks are going bonkers and it does not take much to convince them that they are missing out on some hot action when they hear what they think is another buck giving the tending grunt or the sounds of two bucks fighting.

- If you can, hunt all day. Bucks are cruising for does all day long during this period. If you are going to take a break, do it between about 1:30 P.M. and an hour before sunset. In my experience, this is the period of least movement. I suppose the deer have to rest sometime, even during the chase phase.

9

TREESTAND TACTICS FOR PEAK RUT

Peak rut is when all hell breaks loose in the woods. Does are in heat. Bucks are either tagging along behind a hot doe like a puppy on a leash or feverishly looking for one. Other bucks are tending does and trying to keep less fortunate bucks from making unwanted advances. Some hunters think that peak rut is peak time to be hunting, but I'm not one of them. As far as I'm concerned, by the time the rut peaks, the best is past.

For the past two seasons I have been fortunate enough to draw a non-resident Kansas archery tag. (Now that I've put that in print, I've probably jinxed myself in the lottery for the next decade.) Each season, the only time I have been able to hunt Kansas is during the peak of the rut. If I told you how many bucks I saw during those two weeks of hunting you probably would not believe me. If I told you how many of those bucks were mature deer of three-and-a-half years or older you definitely would not believe me. And if I told you that during those two weeks of hunting, despite the fact that I saw multiple bucks every day and usually multiple mature bucks, I was only afforded two shooting opportunities on mature deer, you would probably deem me incompetent. But that's peak rut for you.

The problem with hunting the peak of the rut is that there is no real pattern to key on. Forget rub lines. Forget scrapes. When a buck is with a doe or searching for one, he could care less about the rest. In fact, that big bruiser you spent so much time patterning in late summer and early fall could be over in the next township right now. Peak rut is when that 12-year-old kid from town sits down on a stump on his first deer hunt, sips a little hot chocolate from the thermos his mom sent along, and two minutes after shooting light has the biggest buck ever killed in your county lying on the ground. Peak rut is when the road hunters whom I despise cruise country roads looking for lovesick bucks brazenly crossing open fields and pastures in broad daylight. Peak rut is the one time of the year when

Big bruisers, like this fine buck taken by Lee Lakosky, are almost always in the company of an estrous doe during peak rut.

anyone, regardless of experience or expertise, might just drop the hammer or the string on the next world record buck. Peak rut is the one time when it definitely is better to be lucky than it is to be good.

So what can you do to maximize your odds of success when hunting during peak rut? For starters, remember this: Bucks are interested in only one thing and that one thing is the opposite sex. Does. Your job is to think doe. More specifically, ask yourself these two questions. Where do the does bed? Where do the does eat? Answer those two questions and you are on your way to having a plan for hunting the peak rut.

Draw it out on paper. I assure you it will make more sense on paper than it will if you try to do the mapping in your head. On one farm where I hunt there are four main doe bedding areas. (See illustration.) There are others I am sure, but I only know of these four. I have stands set up near three of them. I would like to hunt the fourth bedding area as well, but unfortunately, the way it lies, I

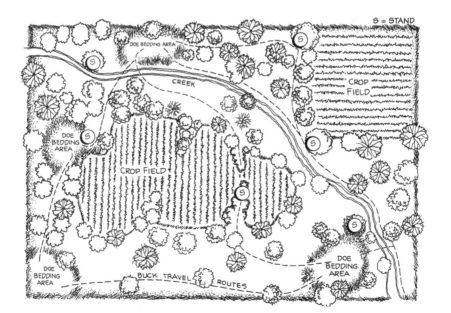

would stand a high risk of spooking any does using the area when trying to get into the stand or when exiting the stand. Rather than take that risk I just do not hunt there. The remaining three areas are prime morning and midday hunt locations during the peak rut.

I map out the routes I think the bucks will use when traveling between bedding areas. When bucks are searching for does in the morning and through the middle of the day they cruise from one doe bedding area to another hoping to encounter an estrous doe at one of the locations. When they make their rounds they will occasionally do dumb things like cross wide open fields, but most of the time, even when smitten by the urge to procreate the species, a mature buck will travel from one doe bedding area to another using whatever cover and terrain features are available to him. For instance, if a mature buck has a choice between walking across a wide-open harvested soybean field to get from point A to point B, or following a brushy fencerow or winding creek bottom, that buck will nearly always opt for the route that provides him with some cover. The other thing to remember in trying to determine the route a buck will use when cruising between doe bedding areas is that a big buck is basically lazy. When I drag myself out of my recliner to get another bowl of ice cream I don't go downstairs, out the back door, around the yard, through the garden, and back up the stairs. Instead, I just shuffle the 20 steps from the living room to the kitchen, get my ice cream, and plop back into the La-Z-Boy. A big buck is the same way. He does not want to expend any more energy than is necessary to reach his destination. If a buck has a choice between climbing straight up and over a steep ridge or slipping through a saddle, he will opt for the saddle. If the choice is between swimming a deep, wide section of the river or tiptoeing across a narrow, shallow riffle below a beaver dam, guess where Mr. Big will cross? If there is a deep ditch or gully in a buck's way, he will likely go around it at the head end instead of crossing where the banks are steep. Think does first. Then think cover and ease of travel.

On the farm discussed above there are two main feeding areas where the does congregate each night. One is a large, harvested cornfield, the other a smaller field. The larger field tends to attract more does than the smaller field, probably because there is more waste corn available. Yet, I have only one stand set up along the larger field, but I've got two along the smaller field. What gives?

What gives is that the big field is so big that it is very difficult to intercept a buck looking for does there. The smaller field, although it attracts fewer does, still draws bucks looking for them and because the field is so much smaller, my odds of being in the right place at the right time are much better here.

Food sources are your best bet for evening hunts during peak rut. I often hunt all day, but rarely do I sit the same stand all day. Instead, I hunt from one of my bedding area or buck travel route stands in the morning until midafternoon, at which time I slip into one of my food source stands.

I employ two strategies when hunting food sources. On larger fields I will often hunt from a stand right on the edge of the field and use a deer decoy or two to try to draw the buck to me. Most of the time, because I can often drive a vehicle near my stand, I will use a buck and a doe decoy. If I have to hike any distance, I don't lug two decoys. I go with a single decoy instead. Peak rut is not the best time for decoying deer, but if you find a buck still looking for a doe or maybe one between does, a decoy will often get his attention. A decoy has to be visible for it to be effective and the farther away deer can spot the decoy the better your odds of having some action.

As much as I enjoy hunting over a decoy, I've got to admit that when you are talking peak rut, a better evening option is to take a stand in cover back off the edge of the field. Sure, you might intercept a buck just by hiking in off the edge of the field a few yards and

Lots of good bucks hit the ground during peak rut, and many serious hunters plan their vacations around it.

hanging a stand any old place, but with a little snooping before you hang a stand, you can up your odds dramatically if you know what to look for in these situations. If a field is being used heavily by does, finding a trail or two entering the field will not be much of a problem. On larger fields there may be a half-dozen or more trails. Young bucks will sometimes cruise these trails as they search for does, but mature bucks don't waste their energy running up and down every doe trail they encounter. They put their noses to the ground and, staying back off the edge of the field, they parallel the field edge and quickly scent check each trail as they cut it. If they detect the scent of a doe about to come into estrous, they take up the trail and follow it. If they do not get a whiff of hot doe, they just continue cruising. These parallel trails usually will be located anywhere from 20 to 50 yards back off the edge of the field. Finding them is not easy, since they are not nearly as well defined as the more heavily used trails entering the field, but look hard and you will locate them. What I look for is a stand location from which I can cover both the parallel trail and a well-used main trail and still be able to shoot to the edge of the field. It is important that you be able to cover the edge of the field because bucks will often walk the edge or just inside the first couple yards of cover where they can easily scan the field for does and scent check any trails they cross. Like I said, it takes some snooping, but once you have found such a stand location, you have found what I think is the best spot in the world to be sitting late in the afternoon during peak rut.

The main reason why so many hunters find the peak rut so baffling is that they find it impossible not to hunt the plethora of buck sign that litters good deer habitat. It is difficult to ignore a cluster of vicious, violent rubs carved into the hide of cedar trees as big around as your leg or a string of big, black scrapes marching boldly down a ridge. Impressive sign to be sure, and if you were not hunting it last week or the week before that, you missed out. But now is not the time to be hunting sign. In fact, many of the best stands I've ever hunted for big bucks during the peak rut had little or no buck sign around them. Do yourself a favor this fall. When you start to see bucks chasing does, abandon that hot sign you've been hunting and start hunting the places just discussed. Your success during peak rut will improve.

10

HUNTING BUCK STAGING AREAS

There was an hour of sun left when the buck arrived on the scene. I first spotted not the deer but a sapling waving wildly in the calm afternoon air. The buck was giving the baseball-bat-thick maple a workout. When he had finished he stepped through a small gap in the brush and I had my first glimpse of gray hide and hard antlers the color of acorn meat. He looked like a good one. Although the buck was only 60 yards away, I needed my binoculars to keep track of his movement in the thick cover of the little flat. I watched as he nibbled at something on the ground before turning his attention to another unlucky sapling. This one held the buck's attention for several minutes. When finished rubbing he again moved slowly in my direction. This buck was in no hurry. It was an hour or more until dark, he had time to waste, and what better place to kill a little time than a favorite staging area.

Staging areas are like the locker room before a football game. The guys are poking fun at each other, maybe doing a little playful pushing and shoving, getting suited up and just waiting to hit the field. Bucks do the same thing. Whenever whitetail deer are feeding in the open, usually in some type of crop field, the bucks tend to hang back in the locker room, or staging areas, waiting for game time near darkness. A big buck might walk into a feeding field well before dusk during the first day or two of the season, but once he gets an inkling that he is being hunted, the odds of catching him out in the open dwindle.

The best way to find staging areas is to follow rub lines. If the rub line is along a trail leading from bedding to feeding areas, and most of them are, there is a good chance you will find a staging area along that route. You will recognize the staging area because it will almost always be in heavy cover and there will be clusters of rubs, usually of various ages.

A common early-season scenario is that a buck has been hitting a certain field with clock-like regularity and then suddenly does not show up for an evening or two. Many hunters mistakenly believe that the buck has found a different food source and they begin the

Look closely and you will likely find a few rubs scattered throughout the staging area.

search for it or just give up on that buck. But a deer does not give up on his main food source that easily. If the does, fawns, and lesser bucks continue to use that field, you can bet that the big boys are still feeding in that field as well, they are just not hitting the field until after dark. On the other hand, if all of the deer quit using a field it is time to start the search for the new food source.

The biggest mistake I see hunters make when deer are feeding in a crop field is that they refuse to quit hunting the field edge stands even after the big bucks have stopped using the field during shooting light. It's like they see all of these other deer using the field and they just can't bring themselves to believe that the big boy won't make his appearance, if not this evening, then surely the next evening. So they sit on the field edge and get to see a lot of deer, but the buck they are looking for is dinking around his staging area. Again, field edge stands can produce a big buck during those first couple days of the season, but once a buck has any idea he is being hunted, my advice is to abandon the field edge stands and find the staging area.

LATE-SEASON STAGING AREAS

If winter weather arrives in time the hunting can be fantastic during the last weeks of the season. Snow and cold combine to force deer to focus on the available food sources, and since those food sources are limited at this time of the year, determining where the deer are feeding is really easy. It is common to see a dozen or more deer using a field in the evening. The big deer have no choice but to use the same fields as all of the other deer because, after the rigors of the rut, they need food just like the rest, maybe even more desperately. But even though they are driven by hunger, those big boys just cannot bring themselves to join the does, fawns, and young bucks at the dinner table until after dark. They hang back in cover and wait for darkness. These late-season staging areas do not differ that much from

The best time to put up a stand in a staging area is during the middle of the day when deer will be bedded down.

the earlier season staging areas and sometimes when the same field is being used, the staging area used in October will be used again in December or January. The biggest difference is that you cannot depend upon rubs to locate these late season areas. Bucks will do some rubbing at this time of the year, but it is minimal. You are going to have to depend upon tracks and droppings for clues.

I like to backtrack along the main trail or trails entering a field. If you find a place along that trail, usually in a thicket, where there are a lot of big tracks and large droppings, there is a good chance that you have found the buck's staging area. Hang a stand and be waiting by midafternoon.

STAGING AREAS AND THE RUT

Bucks know that the best place to find does in the evening and at night is in the fields in which the does will be feeding. Usually, this will be a harvested crop field, food plot, natural meadow, or clearcut. While an immature buck won't hesitate to enter the field to check out the does while there is still plenty of shooting light left, the big boys are seldom so brazen. Of course, when the rut is at its peak it's not unusual to see one of the big bucks cruise across an open field chasing or trailing a doe, but we are only talking about a couple of days when the bucks are that crazy. During the rest of the rut, those bucks will spend some time at staging areas.

In hill country, these rut staging areas will normally be located on a point, bench, or knob, someplace fairly flat and usually above the field the does will be using. I think this elevated position is important. If at all possible a buck likes to be able to sneak a peek at the field to check on the does without exposing himself in the process.

Very often, you will find the staging areas located somewhere along the inside perimeter trail. Bucks spend a lot of time cruising these perimeter trails during the rut. A perimeter trail is a trail that cuts across the trails the does are using when entering and leaving the fields. Look for them to be around 30 yards back from the edge of the opening. By walking the perimeter trail a buck can scent check each of these trails as he crosses the trail. If he smells something interesting, he will follow it.

My favorite location for a staging area stand is when I can find a place where bucks have been staging along a perimeter trail where it crosses one of the major trails entering the feeding area. You've got three things going for you on a stand like this. If the buck is hanging around using the staging area you are in business, but you also might intercept a good buck just cruising through on the perimeter trail or on the main trail.

Most of the time a staging area will be located between 30 and 100 yards back from the edge of the field, but if there is heavy cover in which the buck feels secure, it is not unusual for a buck to stage right on the edge of the field. I have one favorite staging area stand from which I've taken several nice bucks over the years that is the perfect example. This staging area is at the very end of a long, nar-

I like to hang a few scent wicks around my stand when hunting a staging area. Bucks are just killing time and scent wicks will sometimes appeal to their curiosity.

row field, with several fingers jutting into the field. The field slopes from one end to the other and at the high end of the field is a little flat, about the size of a big living room. The flat is all grown up with brush and sumac, but from that little flat a buck can easily survey the entire field for does without ever showing himself. As you might expect that little flat is usually pretty torn up with rubs and scrapes, most of which are just made out of pure frustration. It's a super place for a stand during the rut, and it will be good for many years to come. That's the thing with a good staging area, it will be good season after season so long as the food source that attracts the does remains constant. If the crops in the field are rotated and planted to something the deer do not relish, the staging area might go unused for a season or two, but as soon as the field is planted to something the deer like, they will start using the field and you can bet that the staging area will again become active. I can hang my stands on staging areas in the spring or well before the season and know that when the time is right those stands will see plenty of use.

In fact, early spring, between the time the snow melts and spring green-up, is the perfect time to locate staging areas. Rubs are often the key to finding them. Look for areas with a lot of old rubs of various ages or scars of different ages on the same tree. Rub lines can lead you to staging areas, but don't look for lines of rubs at staging areas; instead, look for clusters. Often you will find scrapes at staging areas, as well. These scrapes are not really calling cards for does like other scrapes; they are usually made by bucks just venting their frustration while they wait for darkness so that they can get into the fields and start harassing the does.

And the buck in the beginning of this chapter? Well, he eventually worked his way to within range of my stand. And, yes, he was a good one, with long sweeping main beams and excellent tine length. And I should have had him, but there was one skinny branch, just a twig really and—well, you know how it goes sometimes.

11

MAGIC PLACES

I really hate hunting the thick stuff. It is hard to see much and the walls kind of close in when the hours mount up. It can also be boring, and it is always, for me anyway, a real test of willpower. One day in a tight-quarters stand is usually my limit, but recently—even though I had not seen a single deer the previous day—I found myself back for a second try because I was convinced that my best chance of scoring on a mature buck on the farm I was hunting was to haunt the best cover on the farm. That cover just happened to be in the shape of 30-some acres of spruce and pine that the landowner had planted nearly 20 years ago. The trees had been planted for wildlife habitat and erosion control, so they were crowded together and never thinned. Now they stood 20 feet high and shoulder to shoulder, forming an almost unbroken sea of dark green. What the old-timers often refer to as being as "thick as the hairs on a dog." Just the kind of place a big buck likes to hang out.

Late in the afternoon on the second day, with nearly 20 hours of staring at the same green walls surrounding me, I was finding it hard to concentrate and finding it even more difficult to maintain optimism for the stand I was hunting. Maybe I should have hunted the perimeter of the stand of evergreens or maybe the oak ridge would have been a better choice; surely I would have at least seen some deer at either place. By the sound of the gun shots I had heard the last two days, other hunters were finding plenty of action in the more open timber. But then I reminded myself that I was not out here to see a bunch of deer, I had come for one very special buck, and everything I knew about mature deer pointed towards the conifer thicket as the best place to make his acquaintance.

Off and on for two days I had used my grunt call and a little light antler tickling to get the attention of any buck bedded in the conifers. So far the only thing I had attracted was a pesky pine squir-

I like the feeling of confidence I have when hunting a stand that has worked its magic for me on past hunts.

rel and a curious bluejay, both of which made a lot more noise than I would have liked once they discovered the source of the racket.

I don't know if the buck responded to my grunt call or not, but I had just tucked it away inside of my coat when I heard a stick crack somewhere off to my left. I shifted the rifle into position and strained to hear another sound while trying to look through that sea of green. Like they so often do, the buck just materialized. At first I saw only the tips of his antlers, then his head and neck, and finally his chest. The rifle bucked and the deer went down. He lay only fifteen steps from the base of the tree in which I sat. Up-close action is the rule when you hunt the thick stuff. Few hunters have the mental stamina to sit it out on such claustrophobic stand sites, which is exactly why these tight places are so good for big bucks.

Many of the encounters I have had with big bucks in tight cover have taken place while I was hunting other game. As a kid, my buddies and I would often hunt cottontail rabbits over a loud-mouthed beagle named Tinker Bell. There were not a lot of deer around the area where we lived back then, but it seemed that every big buck we ever saw was rousted out of some godforsaken bramble patch that even the rabbits had trouble getting through.

Later, while hunting pheasants behind my father's half-broke Labrador, a dog he never could break from running deer, it was not unusual for a corn-fattened, heavy-horned, farm-country buck to come blasting out of some impossible tangle of willow and slough grass with that black demon hard on his hooves. Pa would scream at the dog until he was blue in the face and then we would just sit down and wait for him to come back, which usually took about fifteen minutes. Luckily, there were not nearly as many deer around then as there are now, or we would have spent all day waiting for that dog to come back.

Even while duck hunting I was getting lessons in the places big bucks go to be left alone. Many times on opening day of deer season,

Pa and I would be sitting over a spread of mallard decoys in a big cattail marsh and have a deer or two swim through our decoys. All of them were big bucks. I didn't know it then, but I do now, that those bucks were not just crossing that big cattail marsh to get to another patch of timber; rather they were looking for a dry hummock within the marsh on which they could hide out for the day. Most of those bucks probably died of old age.

Those early experiences were the foundation for my current penchant for hunting big bucks in tight cover. Wherever I travel to hunt the whitetail, the first thing I look for is the nastiest cover available. I suppose that somewhere there might be cover so thick, so thorn-laden, so muddy, so impenetrable that a whitetail refuses to enter it, but if such cover exists, I've never found it.

This, of course, is not news to most whitetail hunters. Many of you hunt the edges of thick cover. Many more hunt the trails, the saddles, and the funnels deer will hopefully use as they travel to and from the heaviest cover. Good places all. But few ever hunt in the thick of it. I don't blame you. It's not fun hunting a place where you can spit about as far as you can shoot. It's nerve-wracking to know that there is a deer within just a few yards of you, to hear the sucking sound his hooves make as he pulls them from the mud with each step, and yet not see a single hair on his hide.

Many times after a fruitless day or two in some hellhole I've vowed never again. But I don't keep my word. It's too late for me. I've seen too much, too many big bruisers twisting and turning their racks as they somehow maneuver through a wall of bramble, briar, and vines. After all of this time, all of those deer, I suppose I should no longer be amazed, but I am.

I only know of one way to hunt these places. You get there early, long before the first glimpse of day, and you claw your way into your stand. Usually, the higher the stand the better because the more holes and pockets you can look down into from your perch, the better the odds that you might just get a glimpse of him. However, there are circumstances when a stand lower in a tree, or even a ground blind, will actually provide better visibility than a stand high in a tree. The most common of these circumstances is when hunting in conifers. Spruce, fir, and younger pines all have heavy, thick branches that droop nearly to the ground. From above, it is sometimes impossible to see down through this canopy of branches, but from ground level you can look beneath the branches where deer travel. Bring along plenty of grub, some water, and if it's cold, extra clothes, because to hunt these places right you are going to be there until dark or until you put that buck on the ground, whichever comes first. If you give up during the day and climb down, you can forget about hunting that stand again the next day. In this cover you can't make a quiet exit. He will know you have been there. Once he knows, he may continue to use the cover, but he won't go near where he heard you. You can bet on that.

Your best chance will come in the first half-hour of shooting light. Big bucks don't hang around the fields and open timber until it is full light like other deer sometimes do. In fact, by the time younger deer have decided it is time to vacate the places where they have fed for the night, big deer are often already in their security cover. Only during the rut will you sometimes catch a big bruiser slinking his way back home in the full light of morning after a long night of carousing with the boys and chasing does. I remember one such buck well, because at the time that ten pointer was the largest buck I had ever taken with a muzzleloader. I remember how surprised I was to see him. The sun had been up for an hour when he came. Reminded me of a teenager trying to sneak into the house after missing curfew. One step, then look, listen, and sniff, another step, then look, listen, and sniff. He knew he was late and he didn't like it. I got the feeling that when the big fifty belched a barrelful of fire, smoke, and hot lead that ten pointer was not even surprised.

The thick stuff really attracts bucks when hunting pressure is a major factor, but you could do worse than to concentrate your efforts there even when bucks are tending does. While a lot of the antics associated with the rut, like the scraping, the chasing, and the trailing, routinely take place in more open habitats, when a buck finds himself a hot doe he will push that doe into a place where he can hide her from other bucks and keep her all to himself for as long as she is responsive to his approaches. What better place to hide out with a favorite girlfriend than some dog-hair thick cattail slough or twisted tangle of briar and bramble?

The second reason why these places are so good during peak rut is that even during the heat of the rut, big bucks are rarely so sex-crazed that they throw all caution to the wind and brazenly go off in search of does through timber infested with hunters. It happens, but not often. Mostly these bucks slink off to heavy cover and sulk and wait for the hunters to leave. But they are not happy campers. These

It is interesting that magic stands often produce several good bucks over the course of a few hunting seasons.

bucks are sexually frustrated. Often, even at midday, I have seen them rise from their beds and take out their frustration on some hapless sapling or paw out a few scrapes just to let off steam. Think these bucks aren't suckers for a grunt call, doe bleat, or rattling antlers?

You might be thinking that using a stand is not the way to hunt these places at all, that a deer drive is the way to go. All I can say is have at it, but count me out. I've tried many times to drive deer out of these strongholds and it just doesn't work. A young buck or doe might get nervous and make a break for it, but not the big boys. A big buck is one cool customer in the face of hunting pressure. One thing that buck instinctively knows is that if he vacates the best cover his odds of living another year have just taken a serious nosedive.

Back when I was just out of high school a group of buddies and I saw a big buck and a doe enter a football-shaped patch of scrub willow and slough grass that was completely surrounded by plowed field. With spirits high, we positioned standers and then commenced to line up and push that five-acre hellhole. A doe broke on the first push. On the second, I killed a nice eight point as he exploded from cover nearly at my feet. On the fourth, the big buck got up just before P.T. would have stepped on him, but tangled in vines, he could not get a shot and the big buck slipped back behind the drivers. On the seventh push through the slough the big buck pulled the same stunt when another member of the group nearly stepped on him. After ten pushes and several hours, sweating, muddy to our hips, exhausted and befuddled, we quit and went looking elsewhere. I doubt we could have forced that buck out of that thicket with twice as many drivers.

I've been hunting the thick stuff for a long time now and I still don't like it. Never having done hard time, I don't know what it feels like when that whistle blows and you are ushered back into your cell, but I suspect it is something like climbing into a stand in the nasty stuff for that third or fourth day in a row. There's nothing aesthetically pleasing about these places, but when hunting pressure is intense, I don't know of a better place to wait on Mr. Big.

THOUGHTS ON TRAILS

Like most deer hunters, I've spent a lot of my time in the deer woods sitting in stands overlooking deer trails. Some of those trails were mighty impressive, too. When you find a trail where the hooves of countless deer have literally chewed away the soil and left not so much a trail as a deep rut, you can't help but anticipate plenty of action. I have to admit I have seen a lot of deer slipping along on these trails. Most have been does and fawns and immature bucks. I'm convinced big bucks rarely travel the same heavily-used trails favored by other deer. Maybe it's because they are smarter or more cautious than other deer, or maybe it's because the biggest bucks don't do much of anything the same as other deer. I don't know, but I do know that if you want a crack at the biggest buck in the neighborhood, sitting in a stand overlooking the most obvious trail in the woods is probably not going to get the job done.

It's not that the big boys don't go to some of the same places as other deer. Big bucks often feed in the same fields, cutovers, or oak ridges, they often drink at the same seep, and they may even bed in the same general area as other deer, but rarely will they use the same trail as the other deer to get from one place to another.

PARALLEL TRAILS

Parallel trails are a good example of this trait. Most deer trails connect bedding areas to food sources. The most obvious trails are those used year after year by generations of deer. These trails are found in places where the food source and the bedding areas do not vary much from season to season, which is common in the agricultural regions of our country.

The illustration shows a common example. The deer bed in the large block of timber, make their way along the creek bottom in

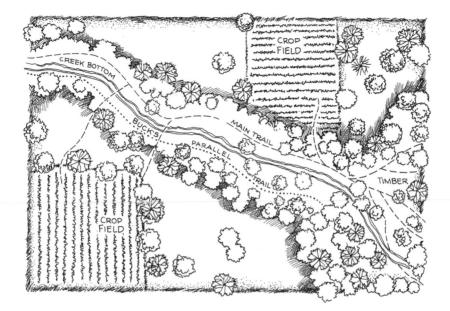

the late afternoon, and filter out into the agricultural fields to feed at dusk. In the morning, they reverse directions. Finding the main trail the deer use in that creek bottom is child's play, but finding the trail the biggest buck is using takes some detective work.

In hill country, the biggest bucks will nearly always travel at a slightly higher elevation than the rest of the deer. On flat ground, you will need to check both sides of the main trail. Sometimes the two trails will nearly touch, but if the terrain allows, the bucks' trail may be 100 yards or more away from the main trail. These parallel trails are not easy to find because one deer, or at the most a couple of bigger bucks, don't leave behind much sign. The grass won't be worn away as it is on the main trail, it will just be flattened. Fallen leaves will barely be disturbed. Look for big, blunt tracks in soft soil, large droppings, and especially rubs. A string of rubs are like highway mile markers. You won't usually get that lucky, but even two or three rubs, along with a track here and some droppings there, maybe some hair on the barb of a fence, and the experienced, imaginative eye begins to see a trail others will miss.

In more open country you may be able to actually spot the deer you are looking for as it slips along a parallel trail. Myles Keller, the archer who has taken more Pope & Young whitetails than any other hunter, spends a lot of time sitting on his duff with binoculars or a spotting scope in hand. Myles has often spent evenings watching deer filter along a main trail on their way to feed, and while he pays attention to the deer on the main trail, what he is really looking for is a big buck using a parallel trail to reach the same destination. "One time I found a place where a good number of deer were bedding in a big willow slough and then moving along the edge of a drainage ditch to reach the harvested cornfield in which they fed each evening," Myles told me. "I sat back on a big hill a half-mile away and watched them through my spotting scope for three evenings in a row and finally on the third evening I spotted a big buck walking all alone along a fenceline that paralleled the drainage ditch, but was probably a city block away from the ditch. On the fourth evening I watched that fenceline again and, sure enough, the ten pointer used the same route again. The next afternoon I was waiting for him. I've taken a number of nice bucks off of parallel trails."

Another type of parallel trail to look for is a trail that parallels the edge of a field or clearcut instead of a main trail. Mature bucks use these trails to check out a field before making their entry into the field. A younger deer, driven by hunger, will often just walk or even run straight out into the field or clearcut, but not a big buck. Empty belly or not, these deer are just too cautious for that. Instead, they pace along the edges, usually 10 to 60 yards back from the edge of the field or clearing. From these parallel trails they let their eyes, ears, and nose assure them that the coast is clear before finally moving into the field, usually well after shooting hours have passed.

TRAIL-CUTTER BUCKS

When the rut kicks in and the big breeder bucks are on the prowl for receptive does, they do not waste their time and energy cruising up and down every deer trail, instead they cut those trails, scent check them, and if they do not detect the passing of a receptive doe, they quickly move on. By doing this a buck can scent check dozens of trails each day. When the buck picks up the scent of an estrous doe, he puts his nose to the ground and takes up the track. This is one of the few times that you will see a mature buck using a well-established deer trail.

In hill country, bucks spend the mornings cutting across and scent checking trails high on ridges. This is probably because the bucks know that the does have already moved off the lower feeding areas and into the higher bedding cover. It's also feasible that rising thermals allow the bucks to scent check for any estrous does in the valleys below them. The bucks move low in evening, anticipating that the does will now be using the trails to move back to the feeding areas. The falling temperatures again send the thermals rushing downhill to the bucks' waiting noses. (See illustration.) Even if you hunt flat terrain, the same concept holds true. Mature bucks will cut trails near the bedding areas in the morning and nearer to the feeding areas in the evening. This is why, at this time of the year, I typically hunt a stand high on a ridge or near a bedding area from first light until early afternoon and then move lower and closer to the feeding area for the evening hunt.

Although bucks are often called ridgerunners, in my experience, bucks do not actually spend much time on the crest of the ridge. They prefer to travel below the lip, often about one-third of the way down from the top, in their search for does.

I'm convinced that a mature buck has a route that he will run in his search for an estrous doe and that he will stick to that route

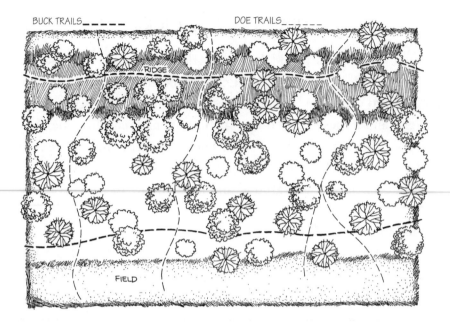

until he encounters a hot doe. In areas where deer are numerous and individual deer have small home ranges, many times I have seen the same buck cutting major trails along the same path several times in one day and often on several days in succession. Where the deer population is low, such as in many areas of the Canadian north, a big buck's route may be so long that he only passes by your stand location once every couple of days. It takes a lot of patience and a strong belief to wait on such a buck, but the rewards are worth it.

This penchant for taking the road less traveled is so ingrained in mature bucks that even when the snow is deep and the going tough for deer, I have often found the biggest bucks making their way through the drifts alone or in the company of another bruiser rather than following the main trails where the going would be much easier. A big buck I killed during Iowa's late muzzleloader season is a prime example of this behavior. A blizzard roared through Iowa on New Year's Eve, dumping nearly two feet of snow that was packed into towering drifts by howling winds. The bottom dropped out of the thermometer as the storm finally moved out and clear skies and gusty northwest winds prevailed for nearly a week, followed by another snowstorm. I hunted all day every day for ten days straight and saw the big buck only twice, once on the first day of my hunt as the heavy-horned brute made his way alone across a snowpacked CRP field to a small patch of standing soybeans where 20 or so other deer, all of which had arrived via a whitetail freeway, were already pawing for the high-protein beans. When he finally got to the field, it was past shooting hours, but I watched him through binoculars for a few minutes and vowed that I would concentrate on that buck for the rest of my hunt. Ten days later I was wishing I had never seen that buck. But with only minutes left in the season, here he came alone again, making his way, as most of the big ones do, along a path less traveled.

FUNNELS

Given an option, most mature bucks will avoid main deer trails and stick to their own. But take away that option and you have a funnel. A funnel is nothing more than some natural or manmade feature that restricts lateral movement. The tighter the restriction the better the funnel. Examples of funnels abound in the whitetail's world, and when bucks are on the move in search of does there is no better place for your stand. Here are some examples of just a few of the many funnels you will find if you look for them.

The brushy fenceline connecting those two woodlots in the top illustration on page 118 is a nifty funnel. So are the points jutting out into ridgetop fields in the bottom illustration on page 118. Some creek bottoms, when viewed from above, display that classic hourglass shape, as in the illustration on page 119. All of these are examples of funnels that could easily be "discovered" from the comfort of your favorite chair before you ever set foot in the woods, just by looking over a topographic map or aerial photograph.

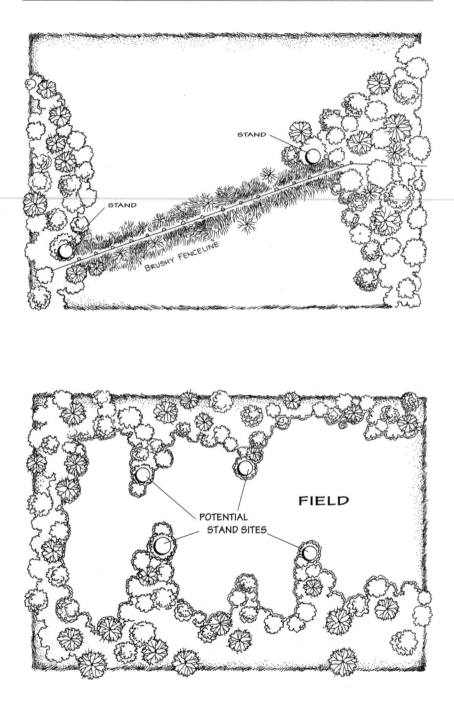

STAND

STAND

BRUSHY FENCELINE

FIELD

POTENTIAL
STAND SITES

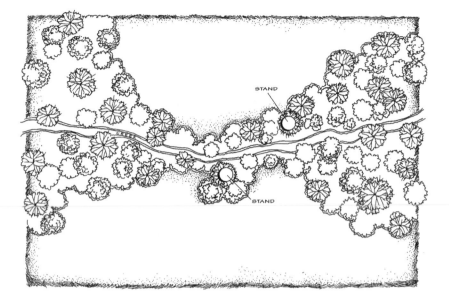

Other funnels, however, can only be found if you get out and hike the property. For instance, there is a ranch I hunt in Kansas where most of the deer are concentrated in a relatively narrow river bottom. One day, while hiking that river bottom timber, I found where a powerline right-of-way dissected the river bottom. I remember thinking that the powerline would have made a great shooting lane for a rifle hunter, but because I was bowhunting at the time, I did not give the 75-yard-wide swath the power company had cleared any more thought until I noticed that the boys on the bulldozers had inadvertently built me one dandy funnel. After all of the trees in the right-of-way had been cut, heavy machinery had been brought in to pile the trees off to one side. The "tree dam," shown in the illustration on page 120, was anywhere from four to seven feet in height and probably ten to fifteen feet wide. A deer could have scrambled over it in an emergency, I suppose, but so far as I could tell none had. Why should they when all they had to do was walk to a gap in

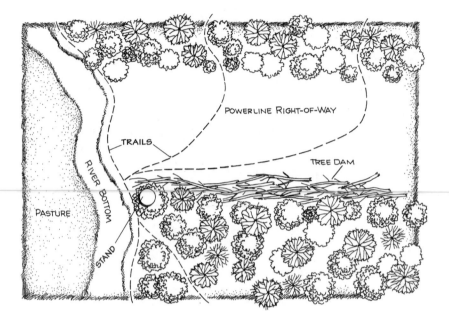

the tree dam and cross there? The best gap I found was on the north end of the property where the tree dam was unbroken for several hundred yards, ending abruptly just a few yards from a willow-lined creek bank. On the opposite side of the creek was an open pasture that deer were reluctant to cross.

One of the deadliest big buck stands I've ever seen, but unfortunately never had an opportunity to hunt, was a stand that my friend Randy Grawe, a bowhunter from western Illinois who has taken an impressive collection of very large bucks, showed me last winter while we were doing some scouting. The farm on which the stand was situated had been sold and Randy was no longer going to be able to hunt it, but what a set-up. Randy's stand, shown in the illustration on page 121, was located on a timbered slope with a crop field above and another below, a common arrangement in hilly country. Deer routinely used the slopes, which are too steep to be farmed, as their travel routes. A stand located anywhere along that

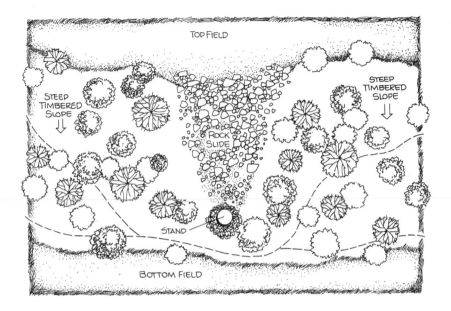

sidehill would have produced numerous sightings of big bucks to be sure, but Randy's stand "squeezed" those bucks into one narrow corridor just twelve steps from the base of the oak in which his stand was hung. A rock slide had made most of the slope impassable, so deer just detoured below the last of the rocks and crossed at that point. Randy told me that he knew before he ever sat in the stand that he had found something special. He was right, and I hope he finds another spot just as good.

Ditches are common over much of the whitetail's range. I'm not talking road ditches, I'm speaking of ditches caused by erosion. The ditch will start on top of a ridge, often at the edge of a field. Heavy rains wash off the field and down the ditch, digging it deeper with each passing year and extending the ditch farther and farther down the slope. The deeper the ditch, the steeper the banks, and the farther it extends down the slope the better. Hike every ditch you come to and watch for deer crossings. Don't worry, you won't be able to miss them. Some ditches will have four, five, or more crossings—forget these, as it leaves too many options. You want the ditch that only has one or two places where the deer cross. You will almost always find one crossing at the very top of the ditch and another at the bottom where the slope begins to flatten out. Either spot could be good, but I'm partial to the tops, as shown in the illustration below. Bucks like to cruise the tops searching for does, and usually the close proximity of the open field adds another dimension to this dynamite funnel. I'm also partial to hunting high because the wind does not swirl as much on top as it does in the bottoms. On the better ones, I put one stand up below the trail and another above so that I can hunt the ditch crossing regardless of the wind.

Everything I just said about ditches goes for creeks, as well. As long as the creek has a fairly high steep bank that prevents deer from crossing wherever they feel like it, you should be able to find one or two major crossings at places where the bank is fairly flat. Some

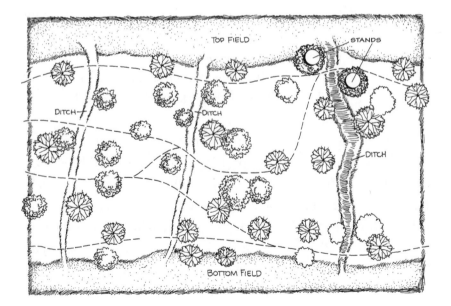

creeks and small rivers are deep enough to discourage deer from swimming across them. Not that deer can't or won't swim, they are excellent swimmers. But give them a choice between swimming a deep portion of the creek or wading across at a riffle and they will take the riffle every time.

It is impossible for me to diagram each type of funnel. I think I have seen every type there is to see and yet I find a new one or two each fall. Hunting funnels has gotten a lot of press over the years and there is good reason for this. In fact, I would have to say that I have more confidence when I climb into a stand overlooking a good funnel than I do in any other set-up.

MAKING YOUR OWN MAGIC

Sometimes you have to make your own magic. Want deer to cross at a particular place along a fenceline? Then obtain permission from the landowner and wire the top strand or two of wire to a lower strand. Deer will quickly find the convenient crossing and use it. Or it might be as simple as opening a gate, again, only with the landowner's permission. Out in Montana one September, David Blanton and I lay sprawled high on a steep bluff and watched deer by the dozens filter out of the willow thickets along the river, cross under, over, or through the barbed-wire fence, and begin feeding on the lush, irrigated alfalfa on the other side. The problem was that the deer were entering the field at a half-dozen different locations. That evening back at the ranch we talked with owner Terry Korman and asked him if we could open a gate that we had seen from our observation post that evening. Since there were no cows in the field, Terry told us to go ahead. The next morning, we opened the gate and hung a fixed-position stand in a cottonwood tree just 22 steps away. Then we left the field alone for two days and went elsewhere to hunt. On the third evening, one of the hunters in our small group hunted the "open gate stand." Over two dozen deer walked through that gate and a half-dozen of them were bucks. An hour before sunset a stocky ten pointer approached the open gate and the hunter sent an arrow zipping through its lungs.

On that hunt, opening a gate worked like magic, but on another hunt, this one in Illinois, closing a gate made all the difference. This time the deer were using the open gate to access a chopped cornfield. The problem was that there was not a tree within 60 yards of the gate and there was no cover for a ground blind. My buddy and I solved the problem by closing the gate and then, with the landowner's permission, creating an easy crossing just 70 yards away where there happened to be a cedar tree big enough for us to place a stand. My buddy killed a nice buck out of that stand two evenings later.

In thick cover you can often get deer to file past your stand by creating easy trails for them to follow. When hunting on their own property some hunters simply use an ATV to make trails through heavy brush, undergrowth, or cattails. Others take it a step further and use a brush hog. But even if you do not have access to machinery, you can get the job done with a saw, machete, and good old-fashioned sweat equity. The key is that the cover has to be thick. In semi-open habitat, deer are less likely to follow manmade trails.

Sometimes, instead of creating trails, I have created detours on existing trails. You can often discourage deer from using a trail, or at least cause them to make a detour that will put them within range of your stand, by blocking a trail. Brush and deadfalls work well for this purpose. Just pile them across the trail so that deer cannot proceed as usual. In the illustration on the next page, the problem was that there were two excellent trails through the funnel I was hunting and I could not set a stand that would allow me to shoot to both trails. Because the upper trail was closest to the open field and I was pretty sure that the deer would not detour around my trail blockade into the open field, I chose to block the upper trail, hoping that I could encourage the deer to drop down and use the lower trail. The plan worked to perfection. Every deer I have seen use the upper trail now just automatically detours to the lower trail where my stand is located before they ever reach the obstruction.

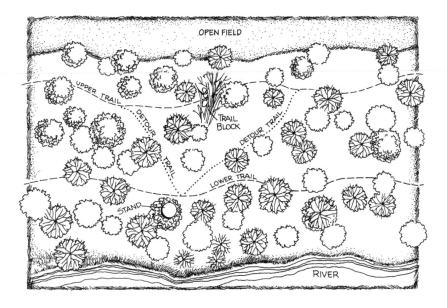

While on a muzzleloader hunt along the Republican River in Nebraska, my buddy Greg Miller and I pulled a dirty trick to encourage the deer to use the trail we wanted them to. We were doing a one-man push of some heavy cover along the banks of the river. We knew that there would be deer bedded in the maze of slough grass and stunted willow, but we had a problem. We only had one hunter to post and there were two main exit routes out of that swamp. We solved the problem by hanging a pair of dirty underwear (I won't say whose they were) from a bush right along the second exit trail. The way the wind was blowing we figured the deer would pick up the scent before they ever got to it, but if not, we hoped that just the sight of those boxer shorts hanging from the bush right along the trail would be enough to cause the deer to have second thoughts about using the trail. While Greg made a long loop around the river to begin the one-man drive, I took up my position behind a double-trunked cottonwood that provided plenty of concealment and a good rest for my muzzleloader. I could see the second trail from my position, but it was too far away for a shot. Fifteen minutes later, I caught movement in the direction of the second trail and with my binoculars I could see a whole string of deer coming through the straw-colored slough grass. They were within 100 yards of that underwear when the lead doe must have gotten a whiff. She slammed on the brakes and 20-some deer behind her followed suit. I could make out three bucks in the string of deer and one, the last one in line, looked like a good one. The deer stood their ground for probably 20 seconds and then began to nervously mill around. Finally, her mind made up, the old doe in the lead brought the whole herd over to the trail that exited the slough right in front of where I knelt behind that forked cottonwood tree. Most of the herd had already filed past me when the biggest buck made his appearance. At only 30 yards, it was just a chip shot and the grain-fattened eight pointer went a short distance and piled up. Greg and I have laughed about the trick we pulled on those deer many times since that day.

12

HIT AND RUN TREESTAND HUNTING

From September until late January, which are the months during which deer hunting occupies most of my time, there are two stands strapped to tie-downs in the bed of my pickup. One of these stands is a favorite climber, the other a lightweight fixed-position stand. These are my "hit and run" stands, the stands I employ when I find smoking hot sign that literally screams out *"Hunt here now, stupid!"*

I won't even tell you how many years I wasted before I finally listened to that message. For many seasons, when I would find an area torn up with fresh scrapes, massive rubs, and pock-marked with big tracks, I made the mistake of growing ever more cautious, instead of bold. Afraid that I would spook the buck that had left the sign, I might hang a stand near the hot sign, but never right where the action was happening. Too risky, I thought. Sometimes, I would hang a stand and then wait a day or two before I actually hunted it, wrongly believing that letting the stand "cool down" for a day or two was the smart thing to do. Caution and patience are good attributes to possess when it comes to hunting whitetail deer, but there are times when immediate and decisive action is called for, as well. Too much deliberation and you might miss the best window of opportunity you will have all season.

In most parts of the country, serious scraping activity will commence in mid- to late October and escalate right up until the time the first wave of does come into estrous, roughly mid-November for most areas. During this same period of time rubs, often dozens of them, magically appear overnight. As the breeding phase of the rut draws near, more and more of these rubs will be of the vicious variety, the ones I call "breeding rubs." You can't miss these rubs. In-

When you know that the time is right for bucks to leave plenty of sign but you are not seeing any from your stand, strap one on your back and go looking.

stead of just rubbing a little bark off the sapling, little, and some not-so-little, trees are simply destroyed. I've seen willow clumps that looked like they had been run over with a brush hog after a mature buck with an overload of testosterone coursing his system got through with them.

A single scrape or a lone rub is meaningless, other than maybe as a visual clue to look for more sign in that vicinity. When I talk about hunting hot sign, I'm talking about a lot of sign. Let me scoot up a tree on a crisp morning in early November and look down on a half-dozen freshly pawed, black-earth scrapes and have the gleam of raw hide on a dozen rubs catch my eye as the sun glints off the oozing wounds and my hunter's blood boils. It's easy to sit all day when hunting sign like that. It's easy to stay attentive and on top of the game. It's easy to remain positive and not give up.

Over the years I've noticed something about sign like I just described. Very often that sign will show up in the same places season after season. The scrapes will often be made under the same overhanging branches. Rubs will appear on trees barely healed from the ravages of last season. New rubs and new scrapes will be added to the mix. Of course, this is not always so; sometimes a really hot area never seems to heat up again. A whitetail's version of a one-night stand, I guess. But enough of these hot areas are used in subsequent seasons that they are worth remembering and certainly worth checking out when the scraping phase of the rut kicks in.

A sprawling valley where a pioneer family tried in vain to clear the hills of timber and plant the sloping land to corn and oats is located on a big piece of public ground in southeast Minnesota. The rains came and washed away their crops and after a few years the family, like so many families, gave up on trying to farm land that was never meant for the plow and moved on to what I hope were greener pastures. All that remains is an old windmill draped in vines and, if you look real close, the limestone foundation of that family's home.

You could never find the root cellar dug into the hill behind the house where the family stored whatever vegetables they were able to raise, but I could show it to you. Once, during a violent early-November thunderstorm, I crawled into that dark, musty cavern hoping that I was not going to be sharing the space with rattlesnakes looking for a denning site for the winter. I've hunted that valley for 30 years and for all of those 30 years bucks have come here to leave their calling cards. When I first found the spot there were a few apple trees, but these are dead and gone now, so I know that it is not the shriveled fruit that attracts the bucks to this place each November. Why they come here I do not know, but I'll bet my favorite bow that once again this fall, the scrapes and the rubs will appear in numbers around the old farmstead. In Minnesota, you cannot leave a stand in the woods on public land, so when I hunt this place I take a lightweight fixed-position stand and a few screw-in steps in my fanny pack and I hike to the place, put up the stand, and hunt for the day. Over the years I have found other places like that long-abandoned farmstead, places where generations of bucks have left their ancient messages carved into the trees and pawed into the dirt. When you find your own, guard its location jealously and hunt it hard when the sign is hot.

Most of the time when I employ hit and run tactics, however, I'm not hunting places where I already know there is going to be good buck sign. Instead, I find the sign through scouting and then hunt it. Let me give you an example.

It was early November and weather conditions were ideal for hunting. I knew that the bucks were on the prowl, checking out the does that were not yet quite ready to breed, pawing out scrapes along the way, taking out their frustrations on little trees, maybe picking a fight with another buck just for the hell of it and basically just acting like bucks gearing up for the annual rites of procreation we call the rut. The problem was that I had been hunting dark to dark for two days and had not seen squat. That just should not happen when you are hunting a good area at prime time, so on the third day, instead of crawling back up into my treestand, I snugged up a pair of well-worn hiking boots, stuck a peanut butter sandwich and bottle of water in my fanny pack, strapped a lightweight stand to my back, picked up my bow, and started hiking the ridges and valleys looking for sign. When I found a rub or a scrape, I looked for more. By midmorning I had covered a lot of ground, but I had still not found what I was looking for. I was making a big loop back to the truck when I hit pay-dirt, and I'll admit that I found that goldmine of buck sign in a place I never would have expected. The part of the big farm I was hunting had been heavily pastured all summer, and although the cattle had been taken off of the pasture in early October, I just assumed that the deer would be concentrated in the thicker woods that had not been pastured and that this was where the bucks would do the bulk of their sign making. But I was wrong.

Because the woods had been pastured and were relatively free of underbrush, the first rubs caught my eye from quite a distance, but I didn't get excited at first because I thought that maybe one of the farmer's bulls had made them during the summer. As I got closer I could see that the rubs were definitely the handiwork of whitetail bucks. They were everywhere. I stood on that ridge and slowly turned in a circle and saw rubs near and far in every direction. Scrapes were less numerous than rubs, but there were certainly enough of them to make it interesting. I followed the ridge for a few hundred yards in one direction looking for the perfect spot to hang my stand. Not finding it, I turned around and marched in the other direction. I found what I was looking for where another ridge inter-sected with the ridge I was on. The intersecting ridge was across the fence and because it had not been pastured it was thick with under-brush. It made sense that deer would prefer to bed in the thicker cover. It didn't take me long to find where the deer had been crossing the fence. Deer, of course, can easily jump a five-strand barbed-wire fence wherever and whenever they want, but if there is an easier way, they will take it. In this case, there was a place where a large branch had fallen from an oak tree and landed on the fence. The branch was heavy enough to push the top strand down nearly to the strand below it and the deer were taking advantage of the dip in the fence to cross. Twenty yards downwind of the fence crossing was a red oak still clinging to some of its rust-colored leaves. Those leaves would help to break up my outline, so I quickly climbed the tree, quietly hung the stand, and settled in to wait.

It would make a neat conclusion if I could tell you that a few minutes later a giant buck appeared and I deftly sent my arrow zipping through his heart, but that is not exactly how things shook out. Instead, I sat until dark in that stand and saw three bucks, two of them little guys, the other a two-and-a-half-year-old buck with four to the side. All three came from the thick stuff, crossed the fence, and went down the pastured ridge. I let them walk. The next day I was in the stand before first light and sat until dark once again. This time I saw five bucks. Three of the five offered me shots, but I passed. On the third day the wind was wrong for my fence-crossing stand, so I took my climber and walked 30 feet up a towering basswood tree I had eyeballed on my original scouting trip for just such an occasion. I could only hunt until noon that day and by ten o'clock I had not seen a single deer and was thinking that my hot spot might have gone cold, but in the next two hours I saw three bucks. One of them was a dandy. The big buck was busy scent checking scrapes as he scurried along the ridge nose to the ground, snuffling for the scent of an estrous doe. It had been raining lightly all morning and the buck made no noise as he hurried along, so I did not hear him, and because he came from hard over my left shoulder I did not see him until he was 50 yards away. I grabbed my bow from the hanger, drew, and grunted with my mouth to stop the buck. If he heard me, he never indicated it. I blatted louder the second time, but the buck just kept his nose to the ground and never broke stride. I prefer not to shoot at a moving deer, but I will if I have to, so I put the pin in front of his chest, swung the bow with him, and released. My arrow ricocheted off a branch halfway to the

Credit: Bast Durbin of Lone Wolf

A lightweight portable stand like this one from Lone Wolf is ideal for hit and run tactics.

buck and went zinging off through the timber. He never even knew he had been shot at.

Even though I had to go home empty-handed after that encounter, this story does have a happy ending. I did not forget about that pastured ridge, and the next November when I returned to hunt the farm again, guess where I went to look for sign? I was not disappointed, either. There were not quite as many rubs or scrapes as the previous year, but there were certainly enough for me. I hung my stand in the same tree I had hunted out of the year before. Even though the branch no longer lay across the barbed-wire fence, the farmer had not bothered to tighten the top strand of wire when he removed it, so the deer were still crossing at the same place. The first day on stand I saw seven deer, three of them bucks, but none of the three were of the caliber I was interested in. On the second morning, I had just finished my first rattling sequence of the morning and hung the horns back on a branch stub when I heard the sound of hooves pounding frozen turf. The buck came the length of the ridge and he came in a hurry, finally skidding to a stop 30 yards away. Backlit by the promise of morning, the steam escaped from his nostrils with each breath. As I settled my second pin behind his shoulder, I could see his sides heaving. Evidently, the mature ten pointer did not much care for the idea of a couple of bucks fighting on his turf and he had come a long way to run the intruders off. He didn't know it, but he had shown up at the wrong fight this time!

WHEN IT'S HOT, IT'S HOT
AND WHEN IT'S NOT, IT'S NOT

Sometimes hot sign does not stay hot for long and it is important that you be ready to hunt the sign when you find it. The next day or next weekend might be too late.

Nobody knows why an area that is littered with scrapes and rubs and crawling with buck activity can suddenly go stone-cold dead. The obvious answer is that does have come into estrous and the bucks have gone off to tend to the does, but I'm talking about a hot area that goes cold before the onset of estrous. My theory is that there are two different types of "hot zones." Type one is the variety we have just discussed: scrape lines and rub lines that more often than not see action for a prolonged period during the rut and are usually re-activated season after season as long as the habitat is not drastically altered. These are the most dependable venues for the hit and run hunter, but they are not necessarily always the best bet.

The second category of hot zone is what I call the "gypsy hot zone." Gypsy as in here today, gone tomorrow, although to be fair, most of the gypsy hot zones I've hunted have been good for more than a single day. How long a gypsy hot zone will produce action depends upon when you find it. If, for example, you discover the hot zone the same day it is being produced, you might be in for two or three days of incredible action, but if you discover the hot zone on day two or three, you might miss out. I should not still be amazed at just how quickly deer can and do vacate a hot zone, but I am.

My guess is that these gypsy hot zones spring up because of the presence of a doe that is in estrous or very near entering estrous. Even though most of the does in any area will be bred during a relatively short two-week span of time, there are always a few that come into estrous early or late. As you might expect when a doe is unlucky enough to enter estrous a week or two earlier than the rest of the does in the herd, that doe is going to attract a lot of attention from the boys in the neighborhood. This, I believe, is what causes all of the rubbing and scraping to be done in clusters rather than in lines, as is more commonly the case when you find hot sign in traditional areas. When you find hot gypsy sign it is not uncommon to find a dozen or more rubs in a space no larger than your home. Scrapes, instead of being laid out in a line along a ridge, field edge, or old logging road, will also be clustered. One scrape will often connect with another and another until you end up with a clover-leaf-shaped scrape no bigger than your kitchen table. One buck makes a scrape, another comes along and paws out his own right alongside the first, a third buck adds his handiwork, and so on. Get enough bucks in on the action and you might find a scrape as big around as one of those backyard trampolines. Numerous small scrapes will be around the main scrape, probably scrapes pawed out by bucks as they await their turn at the main scrape or by bucks not big enough to get a chance to work the main scrape.

Don't confuse these big gypsy scrapes with community scrapes, which are also the work of multiple bucks. Gypsy scrapes are literally produced overnight, will be hot for a day or two, and then probably won't be touched the rest of the season. A good community scrape, by comparison, grows slowly over the course of the season as numbers of bucks continue to visit for the duration of the scraping phase of the rut.

Hit and run is fast-paced, exciting hunting that depends upon finding the hottest sign in your area and hunting it right away.

Early one afternoon during the first week of November, my friend Tom Indrebo, who with his wife, Laurie, ramrods Bluff Country Outfitters in Wisconsin's justifiably famous Buffalo County, was doing some scouting when he blundered into a gypsy hot zone in the making. Two bucks were bedded near a stinking scrape the size of a '56 Buick hood. Both of the bucks were big. Another buck was standing just a short way off and a fourth buck went high-stepping away, its huge white tail flared and wagging defiantly from side to side as Tom approached. The other bucks held their ground, watching Tom walk towards them. They did not move until a doe that Tom had not seen broke from cover and went running up the hill. All of the bucks hightailed it up the hill after the doe. Some hunters would have backed off, not wanting to disturb the area, but Tom Indrebo knows as much about what makes a big whitetail tick as any man I have ever met and he knew what he had to do. He hustled back to his pickup, grabbed a stand and a bunch of steps, and literally ran back to the spot where he had seen all the bucks. While hanging the stand another nice buck came into the big scrape and worked it over. All Tom could do was clutch the tree and watch. With the stand in position Tom climbed down from the tree and went looking for me. He knew that the sooner I got in that stand the better the odds of scoring. But the wind had switched late that morning so I was no longer in the stand Tom thought I would be in, and he was not able to find me. Desperately wanting someone in the new stand that evening, he went looking for another hunter but when he found the hunter he was standing over a dead buck. The hunter thought Tom had some kind of ESP and had come to help him drag out the deer. So the new stand went unhunted that afternoon as Tom helped the hunter drag his buck from the woods. That evening Tom told me about the stand and suggested I plan to hunt it the next day. He did not have to ask twice.

I was in the stand before first light the next morning. When it grew light enough to see, I used my binoculars to have a close look around. Not only were scrapes and rubs visible everywhere, but thanks to a light dusting of snow it was easy to see that there had been a lot of chasing going on during the night. I was pumped, sure that any minute one of those Buffalo County bruisers would come busting into sight. By noon I was not so pumped and considered climbing down and going elsewhere, but then I would look down on that giant scrape and all of those vicious rubs and remember Tom's description of the buck activity he had witnessed at the site only 24 hours earlier and decided that I had better sit it out. At dark, I climbed down. I had not seen a single deer. A dramatic and personally disappointing example of just how fast one of these gypsy hot zones can turn into a gypsy dead zone.

There is an interesting sidebar to this story that is worth remembering when you find yourself sitting in a gypsy dead zone. While I spent that entire day sitting in my stand watching squirrels dig for acorns and chickadees flit from branch to branch, another hunter named Vince was sitting in a stand about 500 yards away watching a parade of bucks paw out scrapes, destroy hapless saplings, and take turns chasing a doe around. Finally, Vince managed to get an arrow through one of the bigger bucks, but that did not put a stop to the buck activity and for the rest of the afternoon as Vince waited for Tom to come and pick him up, he had a front row seat at one of the greatest spectacles any whitetail hunter could ever hope to see. The party Tom had stumbled upon the previous afternoon had moved up the hill. Maybe when Tom spooked the deer the previous day they never returned, but more likely, judging by all of the chase sign I had seen from my stand, the deer had not vacated the area until late in the night. The lesson I took from that experience is that when a gyspy hot zone goes cold, I don't just assume that the party is over. Instead, I assume, until proven otherwise, that the party has simply moved, and in my experience, if the party has moved it has not moved far. Do some looking before you give up; it is often worth the effort.

13

RATTLING, CALLING, AND DECOYING

RATTLING

It was late October in 1968. I don't usually remember dates all that well, but I remember this one because I had been drafted and I knew that the next hunting season would find me in the jungles of a place called Vietnam instead of a chunk of hardwoods in southern Minnesota. What I don't remember is where I ever got the idea to try rattling. Nobody I knew had ever rattled in a buck. Heck, nobody I knew had even tried. I suppose I had read about rattling in one of the outdoor magazines and decided to give it a try. I did not have a set of rattling antlers and I did not want to chop up any of the few intact racks nailed to rafters in the garage. No sense ruining a good set of horns for something that I figured probably was not going to work anyway. So I decided to make do with two complete sets of antlers, skull plates and all.

My "treestand" that morning was the original kind—just a tree. The one I climbed was a giant, old oak with a big limb about twelve feet off the ground on which I could stand while resting my back against the massive trunk of the tree. The oak stood on the corner fence of a sheep pasture, but across the fence was a 40-acre, logged-over section of timber that had grown up into a terrible tangle of forgotten treetops grown through with bramble and briar. Deer loved to bed down in that thicket. I knew this because often in the winter when the Tidemann boys and I would be hunting rabbits in that briar patch, one of us, or more likely Tinker Bell the beagle, would jump a deer or two. The problem was that when the deer got into that twisted tangle they were reluctant to come out. I figured that was where the horns would come in.

My plan that morning was to wait an hour or so after first light to see what I might see and then to make my first attempt at rattling. But patience was not my long suit back then, and when I did not see a deer during the first fifteen minutes of murky gray light, I could not stand it any longer and commenced to beat those racks together. I can tell you from personal experience that using a couple of intact eight-point racks probably sounds pretty authentic, but it is a damn clumsy way to go about rattling. I kept it up for what seemed like a long time, but I suspect it was not even a minute. Then I hung the two skull plates, which I had tied together with baling twine, around a branch stub and jammed my hands back in my coat pockets. I kept scanning that thicket, hoping to see a big, old buck charging out of the thick stuff coming to the sound of my horns, but after a few minutes of seeing nothing I turned slightly on the branch and happened to glance out into that sheep pasture and there he was, a dandy buck striding across that manicured park and headed right for my tree. I panicked and lunged for my bow. Only the fact that the old oak had not yet shed all of its leaves saved me from being picked off by the approaching buck. He closed fast and didn't stop until he was barely 20 yards away. My right leg was jumping like a wild rainbow, and although the limb I was standing on was pretty stout, my unintentional gyrations were enough to make the dried leaves still clinging to that branch rustle against each other with a sound not unlike that a bride's wedding gown makes as she slowly walks down the aisle. It wasn't much. But it was very still that morning and the buck looked up in the tree to see what was making the noise. When he did, I was sure his eyes were locked to mine with instant recognition, although I know today that he probably never saw me. I jerked that old Herter's recurve back with everything I had, a move that caused the buck to do one of those inside-out moves for which the species is famous. It all happened so fast that I'm not sure if I missed him by mere inches or feet, but I suspect yards would be the more accurate measurement. It really does not matter. The damage had been done. The sight of the first buck that ever came to the sound of my clattering rattling horns is forever etched in my mind. Pure excitement. Wonder, too. Up until that moment I did not really know if rattling would work.

As you might expect, I was a rattling fool after that morning. Although I hunted often the rest of that fall, the buck in the sheep pasture was the only one to come to my unique set of rattling horns. I went to war, missed the next season, and came home the following August. I hunted or fished every day but one from then until just after the first of the year. Many of those days were spent hunting other species, but when I hunted deer, my rattling horns went with me. I quickly realized that a buck was not going to come running across a sheep pasture every time I banged the antlers together, but I had just enough action those first few years to keep up my interest in antler rattling.

Since then, I've been fortunate enough to travel extensively in the pursuit of my favorite big game animal. Wherever I go, my horns or some other rattling device goes with me. I've had bucks come to rattling in a bunch of states and provinces and the adrenaline rush still jolts my system each time a buck comes to the horns. Rattling in

Rattling works wherever whitetail deer are found, but it works best in those areas that have a balanced buck-to-doe ratio and a number of mature bucks in the population.

a buck is still pure excitement. That's why I think it is sad that *most* whitetail hunters have never rattled in a buck.

Many have tried, become discouraged, and given up. Others have never even tried. Most are convinced that rattling is something that only works in some exotic location. When I give whitetail seminars on rattling, no matter what part of the country I am in, the most frequent comment I hear is "Rattlin' don't work around here." With that attitude, these hunters are right, rattling never will work for them. But after several decades of horn shaking all across North

America I am convinced that rattling will work to some degree wherever there is a population of whitetail deer. How well rattling will work depends upon the following factors:

1) Buck-to-Doe Ratio

In the world of real estate sales, it is often said that location is everything. Many hunters believe that location is also the key to rattling success. If you are fortunate enough to be hunting a ranch in South Texas or maybe the bush of northern Saskatchewan, then rattling might just work, these hunters figure. But if you are stuck with hunting Missouri, Alabama, New York, New Jersey, Wisconsin, or Pennsylvania, forget it. The truth is that location has nothing to do with how successful you will be in rattling up bucks. A southern buck is as susceptible to rattling as a northern buck and a buck in the east is just as likely to come to the horns as a western prairie whitetail. Nope, latitude and longitude have nothing to do with it, but the buck-to-doe ratio sure as heck does.

The reason why South Texas has developed a well-deserved reputation as the horn-shaking mecca of the world is because most of the whitetail habitat there is under private ownership, the bulk of it in large ranches. Whitetail deer are managed as a cash crop on many of these ranches. Each mature buck is worth X number of dollars. Hunters of means are willing to pay big bucks for a chance at a big buck. To insure that the land is carrying the optimum number of mature bucks, the deer herds are intensely managed in an effort to keep the buck-to-doe ratio as close to one-to-one as possible. Achieving such a perfect balance is nearly impossible, but ratios of one-to-two or one-to-three are common on these ranches. When you have a whitetail herd comprised of one adult buck for every two or three adult does, you are going to have competition between the bucks for breeding rights, and anytime you have competition between bucks, rattling is a very effective technique. If the buck-to-doe ratio is out of whack, as it is in many parts of the country today, there is little or no competition between bucks for breeding rights because every buck has all of the does he can handle and then some.

2) Competition and Curiosity

I look forward to the few opportunities I have to hunt in places where the buck-to-doe ratio is low enough to guarantee competition between mature bucks. Unfortunately, most of the 70 to 90 days I spend hunting deer each season are in places where the buck-to-doe ratio tips heavily in favor of the does. Yet I have rattled in bucks in many of these less-than-ideal locations. Why? Curiosity is often the key. Whitetail deer are just naturally curious critters. When a buck hears what he believes to be two other bucks fighting, pure curiosity will sometimes trip his trigger. I believe this also explains why it is not uncommon to have does come to investigate the sound of rattling antlers.

Why does rattling work so well? It's simple. Bucks fight, occasionally to the death.

3) Perfect Timing

Timing is critical when it comes to rattling success. You might rattle in a buck anytime during the season, but your odds go way up when you present your case during the period when bucks are most likely to respond to your invitation. The exact dates will vary by region, and somewhat from year to year within each region of the country, but the prime period for rattling action is that ten-day to two-week stretch leading up to the first wave of does entering estrous. This is the time period when you want to be shaking those horns every chance you get. This is the stretch during which bucks are gearing up for the big event. Bucks are now on their feet a good share of each 24 hours as they paw out scrapes, make rubs, and roam from doe group to doe group in the hope of encountering a ready doe. At the beginning of this period most bucks that come to the horns will come in slow and wary. But during those last frantic days, when a buck is beside himself with pent-up frustration, I've seen them literally charge in. It is quite a sight to see a mature buck crash through the brush and then come skidding to a halt right in front of you. Unnerving is a good word for it.

Success with the horns tapers off quickly once serious numbers of does come into estrous. In fact, in areas where does far outnumber bucks, rattling now is pretty much a wasted effort. But in regions where there is some competition between bucks for available does, you can enjoy good success by continuing to rattle right through the breeding phase of the rut and even into the first week or so of post-rut.

4) Thick or Thin?

Some horn-shakers say that you should always set up to rattle in heavy cover where a buck will feel most secure coming all the way to the horns. Other hunters claim that hunting relatively open habitat, where you can see a buck coming from a distance, is the ideal situation. Who is right? In my experience, both are.

Where I need that buck within 30 yards or less when bowhunting, I like to do my rattling in heavy cover, unless of course I'm using a deer decoy. The reason I choose heavy cover when rattling while bowhunting is that a buck does not expect to be able to see the bucks he hears fighting until he is right on top of them, so he is less likely to hang up. The problem with heavy cover is that bucks have this irritating habit of circling downwind before committing themselves. To remedy this problem try to set up with a large opening, a river, steep bank, or something else at your back that deer will be reluctant to cross or enter. This will encourage them to circle in front of you instead of behind you.

When I'm gun hunting and can reach out there and touch them at a distance, I could care less if the buck hangs up out there 75 to 100 yards away. So I tend to set up and rattle in semi-open habitat.

5) You Can't Go Wrong

When it comes to technique, all you have to remember is that there is no one correct way to rattle. No two buck fights ever sound the same, so it is not important how you choose to work your rattling antlers. When on the ground, many hunters like to rake brush and pound the ground while working the horns. I do too—sometimes. Other hunters like to grunt, either by mouth or with a grunt call, at the same time as they rattle. The truth is, you can make all of the racket you can muster and you will still never be able to duplicate the cacophony of sounds two mature bucks make when they are really getting it on.

I will say this: most hunters don't rattle long enough. Keep it up for at least a minute or two. Four or five minutes is even better. Give that buck time to make up his mind to investigate.

One word of advice when it comes to technique is to do more grinding than slamming. Whitetail deer do not butt heads like the bighorn rams on that old Dodge truck commercial. Instead, they come together and then grind and twist trying to throw their opponent off balance.

6) Real or Fake?

I've used just about every rattling device on the market to rattle in deer. I'm convinced that when the time is right and the buck is in the mood, what you rattle with makes no difference, that buck is coming. I've had a number of bucks come to the sound of the bell on

Rattle bags don't take up very much room in a fanny pack, so I always carry one with me.

my hunting dog's collar. I know two guys who have rattled in bucks by clattering a couple of aluminum arrows together. And we've all heard the stories about the buck that came charging in while a hunter was rattling the chain on a stand as he attempted to hang it.

With that said, I do still prefer a real set of antlers over all others, but I think it is more of a confidence thing than anything else. I've used my rattling antlers a long time and I've got faith in them. They feel good in my hands, like my favorite bow or hunting knife. And nothing sounds as much like the real thing as the real thing.

My rattling horns are fairly large and heavy and inconvenient to carry, but during peak periods I usually carry my rattling horns anyway. But at other times of the year, when I'm not really anticipating any heavy-duty rattling, I rely upon an H.S. rattling bag. Many times I have rattled in deer when I had no intention of doing any rattling that day. I could not have done that if I had not been in the habit of carrying some type of rattling device with me on every trip to the woods.

By the way, when calling on windy days or when you really need distance, the plastic calls like those sold by Lohman and M.A.D. carry better than real horns, bags, or fake antlers.

7) Tie Them Up

When hunting from a treestand, tie your rattling antlers to your pull-up rope after you are settled in your stand. If you are working the horns and a buck comes in and catches you with the horns still in your hands (this is the voice of experience talking) you can just pitch the antlers to the ground and grab your gun or bow. Another neat thing about this trick is that if the buck hangs up out of range or behind some cover, just jiggle the rope and the antlers will clatter together at the base of your tree. Not only will this encourage the buck to come on in, but now his focus is on the ground and not up in the air.

If you have never given rattling a try, make this the season that you do. If you are one of the tens of thousands of hunters who have tried rattling but given up on it after not having any results, I encourage you to take the suggestions I've shared here and try rattling again. Having a buck come to the horns is just too big a thrill for any whitetail hunter to miss.

CALLING

Every bowhunter I know, and most gun hunters, carry a grunt call with them into the woods. But only a small percentage of deer hunters have ever called in a deer. The main reason for this is that opening weekend of the firearms season is when the highest percentage of hunters with a grunt call strung around their neck are in the woods, and opening weekend of the firearms season is the worst possible time to try to call up a deer. Look at it this way: If someone was in your home trying to shoot you and your phone rang, would you take time to answer the phone?

So you can forget about calling deer anytime hunting pressure is significant. That does not mean that you cannot call in a deer on opening day or any other time during the season. Twice I've found myself hunting virtually alone on opening day of firearms season, and if you are lucky enough to have the same experience, then a grunt call can be a deadly tool. In most places I've hunted, though, the opening weekend is pretty much a zoo and my call stays in my pocket.

When hunting with a shotgun, rifle, or muzzleloader I consider the grunt call to be most effective in heavy cover where my visibility is limited. A few grunts or doe bleats might just bring a buck out of the brush where I can get a crack at him. In more open terrain a grunt call is of less value because you can usually see farther than a deer can hear the call. However, on a couple of occasions I have used a grunt call to get the attention of a buck that was

Whitetail deer have a wide range of vocalizations that they use to communicate with each other. Luckily for us, we only have to know a few of them to successfully call deer.

out of range of my muzzleloader. One buck just stopped and stared and then continued on to wherever he was headed, but the other made a fatal mistake and made a hard right turn to come to investigate the grunts he had heard. In my experience, that's about the norm; half of the bucks that hear it will respond, the other half will not. (This is a season-long average; the ratio gets a lot better when the rut is in progress.)

I've lost count of the number of bucks that have responded to my calling while bowhunting. Dozens of them, anyway. Some I shot, most I let walk, but all were exciting. Anytime an animal comes to the call, whether it's a coyote racing to a dying rabbit, a honker gliding into the decoys, a red-eyed bull elk challenging my bugle, or a buck slipping in to investigate my grunts, it's exciting, heart-pumping stuff. For the bowhunter, I consider the grunt call to be an invaluable tool.

When I first began using a grunt call, like most hunters back then, I used it only on deer that I could see. This was good education because when you call to a buck you have in sight, you can see how the deer reacts to various cadences and volume. After I had called in a few bucks with the grunt tube, I gained confidence in it and began to "call blind," which just means that I would send out a few grunts even when there were no deer in sight. I have no way of estimating how many more bucks I saw because of calling blind because I cannot prove that I would not have seen those same bucks even if I had not been calling. But I believe that calling blind probably accounts for around 20 percent of my buck sightings in a year.

The thicker the cover, the more I call. My theory on this is simple. Let's say that I am sitting in a treestand and can see about 50 yards in all directions. Any deer within that 50 yards I should be able to see or hear, but on a calm day a buck can easily hear a grunt call a couple of hundred yards away. If I cut loose with a series of grunts every fifteen minutes or so, there is a good chance that sometime during my stint on stand those grunts are going to reach the ears of a buck that is within hearing distance of the call but not within my 50-yard sight zone. Simple math.

Calling works from opening day right up until the last bell and I've personally called in bucks during the months of September, October, November, December, and January, but there is little question that calling works *best* during the rut. From the time they begin rubbing and scraping right up until the last doe has been bred, a buck is often a sucker for a buck grunt or a doe bleat. It makes sense. A buck only has one thing on his mind during the rut and when he hears another buck grunt, odds are excellent that he will come over to see if that buck has a doe with him that he just might be able to run off with. Over the years, while calling to bucks I could see dur-ing that two-week period before the does are in estrous, I have had at least 75 percent come to the call. That figure begins to drop when bucks are trailing or tending a doe. It is not impossible to call a buck away from a doe, but it does not happen very often.

The whitetail deer has 20-some different vocalizations that it uses to communicate with other deer. Luckily, you and I do not need to learn the entire language. The contact grunt, the trailing/tending grunt, and the doe bleat are all you really need. Today, thanks to the availability of variable-tone deer calls, you can make all three on the same call. I'll warn you, however, that not all deer calls are created equal. Some sound more like recycled duck calls, others are too tinny, and still others require too much air pres-sure to activate. Some variable-tone calls require that you take the call apart and adjust a rubber band on the reed to change over from a buck grunt to a doe bleat. Some of these calls sound great, but I

Variable-tone calls like this Tru-Talker can be made to sound like a small buck, doe, or mature buck just by manipulating finger pressure on the enclosed reed.

like a call that allows me to change the pitch, the volume, and the sound without ever having to take my eye off the deer.

Whatever brand of call you own or purchase, the best way to learn how to make the contact grunt, tending grunt, and doe bleat is by listening to an instructional tape and then duplicating what you hear. I know that there are many hunters who have never tried a grunt call because they have had trouble learning to use a turkey call or duck call and just don't think that they will be able to master it. Please don't let that stop you. Learning to make the three vocalizations just mentioned on a good grunt tube is child's play when compared to learning to call turkeys, ducks, or elk. Trust me, it's easy.

The contact grunt is a low-volume, single-syllable vocalization, which to my ear sounds like *urrp*. Both bucks and does make the contact grunt, although bucks tend to make it more often, and the buck's contact grunt is louder than the doe's. I've heard bucks making the contact grunt during all months of the season, but in my experience it is used by bucks more often during September and October than it is during the rut or after the rut. There is no aggression in the contact grunt and it does not appear to be a strident request for communication with other deer. I've often seen bucks just moseying along through the woods minding their own business and occasionally, seemingly for no reason, giving a contact grunt or two. The contact grunt appears to be a whitetail's way of saying, "Hey, I'm over here, is there anyone else around?" Often, when a buck hears another buck make a contact grunt it will walk over to investigate. I've watched many bucks come together because one or both of them have emitted contact grunts. None have been aggressive towards each other, although there is often a little playful sparring and pushing around. I believe that the contact grunt could just as easily have been termed the "curiosity grunt" because it appears to me that a buck responds to a contact grunt more out of curiosity than anything else. I guess the real point to hunters is not why the contact grunt is so appealing to bucks, but just that it does work and works well. In fact, the contact grunt works so well, especially prior to the rut, that I can recall only a handful of bucks that I could see and that obviously heard my contact grunt and did not respond to the call. That, my friends, should make a grunt call a good investment, even if you never use it for anything but making contact grunts.

The trailing/tending grunt is everything that the contact grunt is not. It is louder, more insistent, repetitious, and made by bucks with only one thing on their minds—sex. Sometimes they are on the scent trail of a doe, other times they have the doe within sight and are giving chase, or in the case of the tending grunt, they have an estrous doe and are planning to stay with that doe until she cycles out. In all cases, you can bet that there is a doe in the picture somewhere.

I hesitate to offer instruction on how to make the trailing/tending grunt because unlike the contact grunt, which sounds virtually the same from all bucks, the trailing/tending grunt varies from individual to individual. I also believe the tone, cadence, length, and volume vary within individual bucks according to what mood they are in at the time. You might think that this lack of focus would make it difficult to produce authentic-sounding trailing/tending grunts, but I suspect just the opposite is true. Because the bucks themselves offer such a variety, you really can't go wrong. Some hunters tend to go with long, drawn out grunts, which in print would go something along these lines: *uuuuur-rrrrrrrrp . . . uuuuuuuuuuurrrrrrrrrrrp . . . uuuuuuurrrrrrrrrrrp.* I usually go with a string of shorter, more abrupt grunts, something like this: *uurrp . . . uurrp . . . uurp . . . urrp . . . uurrp . . . uur . . . uuurp . . . uuurrp.* I might cut it off after a half-dozen grunts or I might run it on for 20 or more, mostly depending on what I feel like doing right then. Like I said, you can get real individualistic with the trailing/tending grunt because the critters you are trying to imitate sure do.

The trailing/tending grunt might bring in a buck anytime during the season, but it is most effective from the time a buck begins pawing out scrapes up until the bulk of the does are in estrous. I've called in a few bucks with the trailing/tending grunt during the peak of the rut, but not many. Bucks that would have stumbled all over themselves coming to the same call just a week prior to the peak are now usually too busy to be messing around responding to grunts. Once the peak is over and the bulk of the does have been bred, however, is again prime time for the trailing/tending grunt. The biggest, most dominant bucks do most of the breeding in a reasonably well-balanced herd and these big boys take their jobs very seriously. After ten days or so of non-stop action they are not quick to give up on their duties for another year, and the sound of another buck trailing or tending a doe is often more than they can stand.

The doe bleat vocalization is one that few hunters use, and I'll admit that I have been slow to warm up to it myself. However, I am more convinced with each passing season that there are periods when the doe bleat is the very best call you can use. During the peak of the rut, the period when the majority of does will be bred, a doe bleat, or a doe bleat in combination with the trailing/tending grunt, is in my estimation the very best call you can use to get the undivided attention of a buck that is between does. The added sound of doe bleat confirms that there is definitely a doe in the picture, while the sound of a trailing/tending grunt without a doe bleat does not. It may be more complicated than that, but I doubt it.

I do know that after years of being frustrated at my inability to get the attention of bucks during the peak of the rut by either grunting or rattling—and I'm speaking here of bucks that were not with does—I reluctantly turned to doe bleats. Don't ask me where my bias against doe bleats originated, I cannot recall, but it was there and I know today that this unfounded bias cost me some good action over the years. The doe bleat is not magic. It does not work all of the time. In fact, it does not even work most of the time. But it works when nothing else will and that is reason enough for me.

One of the great things about calling is that it will work at any time of the season in any kind of weather.

There are two ways to make doe bleats (often called estrous bleats) and both are easy. One is to use a good variable-tone grunt call. I happen to use an H.S. Tru-Talker. With the Tru-Talker I can instantly switch from a buck grunt to a doe bleat just by shifting finger pressure on the reed of the call. Other variable-tone grunt calls have plungers or buttons that you push depending upon what sound you want to make or a rubber band on the reed that can be moved. All will work.

The second way to make the estrous bleat is with what I call the "call-in-the-can," produced by Primos, Quaker Boy, and probably several other call companies. These cans are simple to operate. Rotate the can and it emits a very realistic doe bleat. Using a can makes it easy to mix a few doe bleats in with a series of grunts, creating a very realistic impression to any buck within earshot.

Here are a few calling tips that I know will greatly increase the number of deer you call into range:

- I'm always hearing and reading advice that warns against calling too much. Solid advice for some situations, but not for all. The truth is that no two situations are alike and how much you call should hinge on variables such as habitat, terrain, weather, and the stage of rutting activity, not on some blanket commandment. In a nutshell, I tend to call more often when hunting in thick cover than I do in open timber, more often in hill country than on flat ground, more often in nasty weather than in nice. Anytime I am in a situation where a buck could easily slip by within 100 yards of me without me ever knowing he was there, I call a lot. I also call much more often during the rut than at any other time.

- When a buck is headed your way, tuck away the call and get ready for the shot. There is no need to call again unless the buck for some reason begins to wander off. If a buck stops and stares, don't panic and think you should call again; that is the worst thing you can do. A whitetail is not quite as adept at pinpointing the source of a sound as is a wild turkey, coyote, or bull elk, but they ain't bad either. Get the buck's attention and then let him hunt you.

- Okay, I know that most of you are going to ignore the last one, so if you must call to that buck again, at least try to do it when he is not looking in your direction.

- Don't give up. Calling is easier and more productive than rattling. It works everywhere, with less regard to herd composition, buck-to-doe ratios, and all of the other variables.

I would guess that during the past 20 years I have probably called in 300 deer and, if anything, I suspect that number is on the conservative side. Obviously, I did not kill all of those deer, but I am talking about deer that responded to my call and came close enough that I either passed, killed, or missed. Of those deer, I'm certain that a percentage of them would have eventually ended up within range even if I had not called to them. Let's say 25 percent, or if you are a real pessimist, go ahead and make it half. That still means that I had the thrill of having 150 more deer (mostly bucks) within range of my stand than I would have had without the call. I rest my case.

DECOYING

When Mr. Big stepped into the small alfalfa field, I knew it before I could see him. There were 17 other deer in the field at the time, does, fawns, and a couple of immature hoping-to-get-lucky bucks pestering the does. When all of them suddenly stopped what they were doing and stared towards a dip in the field, I knew that they had their eye on something special. He was special alright. I've spent more time in the places whitetails call home than most, and I've seen only three bucks of his caliber. He looked like a sumu wrestler crashing a midget convention when he stepped into that field.

The buck was about 200 yards away from where I perched in an elevated treestand at the far corner of the field. I grunted to get his attention, but if he heard the grunts, he ignored them. I didn't dare risk rattling; there were too many other deer between me and the big boy and I was afraid one of them would spot the movement and sound the alarm. So I depressed the reed on my call and produced my best rendition of an estrous doe in desperate need of attention. It must have been pretty good, because the buck stopped in mid-stride, looked in my direction, spotted my decoy, and headed over. That's when my right leg began to jump. This is not an uncommon occurrence for me, but it usually happens after the shot, not before. But then this was no ordinary buck.

While I fought for control of my nerves, I told myself two things over and over and over again. "Pick a spot and don't look at those horns." Once, many years ago, when I first began bowhunting, a heavy-horned Minnesota non-typical had ambled down the fenceline I was hunting and passed within spitting distance of the box elder tree where I was standing on a mostly horizontal branch about ten feet off the ground. When I drew back the recurve and released, my cedar arrow went right where I was looking, clattering around in that mass of bone atop the buck's head before falling harmlessly to the ground. I was not about to repeat that mistake.

The buck never broke stride as he closed the distance. He was at 20 yards, walking straight in, and everything (except that jumping right leg) looked perfect. Then I heard the sound of deer running hard in the timber to my right and a second later a doe burst out of the woods and blew into the alfalfa field with a scrubby little buck hot on her tail. As they dashed past the big buck, he simply turned around and walked directly away from me. I drew and grunted with my voice. The buck stopped and turned his head, but he would not turn his body to give me the shot I needed. A few more steps and I stopped him once more, but again he did not present me with the shot. The little buck and the doe had also skidded to a halt when I had grunted the first time. When the big boy fixed his gaze on that little buck, the youngster slunk off like a whipped dog. He then turned his attention to the doe. When he turned to approach her he was broadside at what I estimated to be 40 yards, but in the fading light I misjudged the range and my yellow and white fletching slipped just under his massive chest. The buck was so focused on the doe that he paid no heed to the arrow diving harmlessly into the alfalfa beyond him. When he was gone, I had to sit down before that dancing right leg propelled me right out of the stand!

While I didn't connect on the big buck, that episode, which took place in the rugged hill country of southwest Wisconsin, is a perfect example of why I love hunting over a deer decoy. Action. Hunting over a decoy is fun, not to mention the fact that a decoy will afford you shots at deer that otherwise would never present you with the opportunity.

Decoying deer is easy, too. No matter where you hunt, if there are whitetails around, they can be enticed to pay a decoy a visit. It does not matter if you hunt a 40-acre woodlot in New Jersey, a suburb of Chicago, the big timber of upstate New York, the cornfields of the Midwest, the prairies of Kansas, or the piney woods of the Southeast, decoying will work.

Having a buck like this come into your decoy will hook you for life.

Even though decoying deer is easy, there are mistakes you can make while decoying that will cost you. I've been using a decoy for a long time and I've made most of those mistakes. I'll share those mistakes and pass along some tips that will make using a decoy even more enjoyable and productive for you.

Decoy Placement. Bet you thought I was going to begin with choosing the right decoy, didn't you? Nope, and the reason why is because how you position the decoy is more important than which decoy you use.

In all cases, the wind should be blowing from the decoy to your stand or at the very worst a crosswind. Attempting to hunt over a decoy with the breeze blowing from you to the decoy, no matter how careful you are about odor control, is just asking for trouble.

Position the decoy 10 to 20 yards from your stand. That way if the deer happens to hang up beyond the decoy, which a few are going to do, chances are good that the deer will still be within your range.

When using a buck decoy, face the decoy towards the stand. I know that you have heard and read that you should never face a decoy towards the stand. The reason always cited for this erroneous advice is that when a deer sees another deer staring in one direction it will look in that direction also and may spot you. The only thing I can say about this information is that it was probably passed along by someone who has very limited experience with decoying deer. Every hunter I know who is serious about decoying, faces a buck decoy towards the stand. When a buck approaches a buck decoy, it will nearly always circle around the decoy and come in head-to-head or at least head-to-shoulder. If the decoy is facing your position, the buck will provide you with a perfect broadside or quartering shot.

With a doe decoy, the opposite is true. Face the doe decoy either directly away or quartering away. A buck will usually approach a doe decoy from the rear.

Visibility. For maximum effectiveness a decoy should be visible from as great a distance as possible. The farther a deer is from the decoy when it first sees it, the better the odds that it will commit. Field edges are ideal. Dried-up sloughs, clearcuts, cutlines, and fencelines are other good options. A decoy will work well in relatively open stands of mature timber or woods that have been pastured. In heavy cover, where a deer is going to be right on top of the decoy before it can see it, a decoy will startle more deer than it will attract.

Timing. Whitetail deer are social creatures, so a deer might investigate a decoy at any time during the season. However, the most consistent action over a decoy will occur during the rut. The very best period, in my experience, is the ten-day to two-week stretch just prior to the first wave of does coming into estrous. This is the scraping phase of the rut and it is during this time that bucks will go out of their way to investigate the sound of grunt calls and rattling, which I commonly use to draw a buck's attention to the decoy. Running a distant second is the actual breeding phase of the rut. You can still decoy plenty of immature bucks during this period, but be warned that most of the big boys are with the ladies and are not likely to give up on the real thing for an encounter with a fake.

Odor Control. A decoy that smells like a human won't cut it. To prevent contaminating my decoys with human odor I wear rubber gloves or heavy, clean canvas gloves when handling them. Once the decoy is in position, I spray down the entire decoy with a liquid odor neutralizer.

Adding Scent. You don't need scent to attract deer to your decoy, but I believe the addition of scent will hold deer around your decoy longer, which gives you more time to make a good shot. I don't like to use scent directly on the decoy. Instead, I take a stick and jam it in the ground beneath the decoy. On the stick I hang an absorbent scent wick and apply the scent to the wick. I usually use a doe-in-estrous urine when using a doe decoy and a buck urine or tarsal gland scent when using a buck decoy. If I have access to a fresh tarsal gland I will drape the tarsal gland over the stick. Some hunters like to rub a slice of apple or the meat of an acorn on the noses of their decoys for a little added attraction.

Be Careful. I would not go so far as to say that a decoy should *never* be used when a firearms deer season is in progress, but there are very *few* instances when using a decoy during a firearms season is completely safe. Only you can make that determination.

The Right Decoy for You. There are a dozen different deer decoys available and with their popularity on the rise, you can bet that new models will be forthcoming. The best decoy depends upon a

Silhouette decoys are easy to carry and work surprisingly well.

number of factors, none of which are going to be identical for every hunter.

Before purchasing a decoy ask yourself these questions: (1) How much can I afford to spend? You can purchase a decoy for under $100 or plunk down nearly a grand. (2) How important is portability? If you are going to be hiking long distances to reach the places where you can use your decoy, you don't want a 3D decoy. Silhouettes like the Mel Dutton decoy are light and easy to carry. The Montana decoy is the lightest of all; you can fold it up and stick it inside your shirt. Silhouettes are not as effective as full-bodied decoys, but they are a whole lot more effective than you might think. I use them a lot when I hike into distant stands. If I can drive near to or right up to my stand with an ATV or pickup, I'll go with a full-body. If hunting the evening I'll try to drive in and drop off my decoys at midday. If hunting the morning, I'll go in the day before and stash the decoy in a deadfall or brush pile. (3) Do you consider motion to be vital? Consider installing a Tail Wagger on your decoy. For the ultimate in both movement and realism, the Robo-Coy by Custom Robotics is unmatched, but you will pay for this deadly combination.

Don't let another season slip by without giving decoying deer a try. It's fun and it works.

14

USING SCENTS

When I was just a little fellow, my Grandpa Hank had a big Hereford bull named Curly. As bulls go, Curly was a gentle soul, but gentle or not, getting Curly to go where Grandpa wanted him to go was something of a chore, unless there was a good-looking heifer involved. So Grandpa put a big, brass ring in Curly's nose. After installing that nose ring, Grandpa could walk that ton of hamburger around like a poodle on a leash.

I can't seem to get close enough to whitetail deer to clamp a ring through their nostrils, but I can still lead them by their noses. Deer scents are the next best thing to a brass ring.

Most articles you read about the use of deer scents begin with the author trying to convince the reader that deer scents are legit. I'm tired of playing that game. When used correctly, deer scents work. They don't work 100 percent of the time and they won't make up for slipshod hunting tactics, but I've been using deer scents since the '60s and I've seen enough to convince me that when used appropriately deer scents help me see more and bigger bucks. There is no reason why the proper use of deer scents will not do the same for you.

GROUND TRAILING

An old-timer once told me that the reason big bucks so often walk through the woods with their heads low to the ground is because their racks are so heavy they can't hold their heads up all of the time. The guy was dead serious. He was also dead wrong. The real reason you so often see bucks cruising along in that head-low pose is because they are using their noses to sniff for any ground scent that might indicate the presence of a doe in estrous. When a buck picks up the scent of a hot doe, he will put his nose to the ground like a beagle on a bunny trail and do his level best to follow that tantalizing scent to the source. Why not give them something to trail?

Laying down a scent trail on the way to your treestand is like buying an insurance policy.

166

Laying down a scent trail is easy. I usually use a combination of interdigital gland and doe-in-estrous urine, regardless of the time of the season. A scent trail is most likely to be followed by a buck during the rut, but I have had bucks follow scent trails of doe-in-estrous two months prior to the rut and up to two months after the peak of the rut. A buck is ready, willing, and able to breed as soon as he sheds the velvet from his rack and remains in that state until he drops his antlers. If a buck gets a whiff of a hot doe, it does not matter if it is September or January, there is a good chance he will attempt to find the source of that inviting smell.

A drag rag, which is nothing more than a clean rag tied to a length of twine that you drag behind you as you walk to your stand, works fine for laying down a scent trail. Just be sure to stop about every 50 yards and add a little more scent to the rag so that the smell gets stronger, not weaker, as you get closer to your stand. If you want to go high tech, there are dozens of commercial scent applicators designed to help you lay down a scent trail. Some of the better ones lay down the same amount of scent with each step, eliminating the need to stop and freshen the scent. Or you can use my favorite, a fresh tarsal gland. Wear rubber gloves to carefully peel the tarsal glands from the inside of a buck's hind legs. I take both tarsals and place each into a Ziploc bag. If the rut is in swing and the tarsals are dark and rank with the buck's urine and musk, I leave one tarsal as is, and add about one-half ounce of doe-in-estrous urine to the bag with the other tarsal. I drag them both as I hike into my stand and then hang them on a bush or branch near my stand. Be sure to tie them securely. Several times, when I have not followed my own advice, I have had bucks that I decided not to shoot hook the tarsals and the twine with their antlers until they became tangled and then watched helplessly as they left with my tarsal glands dangling from their racks. I even had one buck spend a lot of time licking the tarsal gland, which is not unusual by the way, and eventually take it in his mouth and walk off. Another time, I watched as a buck went ballistic over a doe-in-estrous-soaked tarsal I had hung from a nearby bush, thrashing the bush with his thin, eight-point rack until he dislodged the tarsal, at which point he proceeded to stomp and paw it into the dirt for a good five minutes. It was quite a show.

Regardless of what you use to lay down the trail, be sure to start far enough away from your stand to do the most good. For some reason, many hunters are under the mistaken impression that a couple

Putting scent wicks in a circle around your stand might draw a buck to you, but more importantly, the scent will likely hold any buck long enough for you to get a good shot.

hundred yards is about as long as a scent trail should be. I don't buy that. As long as the trail is unbroken, a buck can and will follow a scent trail for much longer distances. Since the whole idea of a scent trail is to lure bucks you probably otherwise would never see, the longer the better is my motto when it comes to scent trails. I prefer to lay down a scent trail crosswind to my stand, or I come in from downwind but well off to one side of the stand then loop in crosswind the last couple hundred yards.

Here are a few key points to remember when laying scent trails:

- Scent trails must be unbroken to be effective. A gap of only a few yards is enough to cause a buck to lose interest and head off in another direction. If you use a scent applicator that attaches to your boot, wear one on each boot.
- Don't scrimp on the scent. It is better to dilute the scent and lay down a generous amount than to use only a few drops of full-strength scent.
- Spray your boots with an odor neutralizer to insure that you are not leaving human scent. Some hunters drag the scent rag off to one side of their own tracks to decrease the odds of a buck picking up any scent.

AIRBORNE SCENT TRAILS

Airborne scent trails are not as dependable as ground trails because of the vagaries of wind and thermals. Scent dissipates faster in the air than on the ground. One morning, through my binoculars, I watched a buck that was crossing a dried-up slough suddenly stop, raise his head, and repeatedly lick his nose, a sure sign that he was trying to concentrate an interesting odor. Once he had the direction the buck turned and with head high came directly to my stand. I did not have a rangefinder with me, but I know that the buck was at least 300 yards away when he first detected the airborne scent from the scent canisters I had placed around my stand that morning. My log reminds me that conditions were ideal for scenting that morning. There was a light, but steady breeze, and since the buck arrived on the scene just shortly after first light, the air had not warmed enough at that hour for thermals to influence the air flow. I suspect that conditions have to be ideal, as they were on that morning, for airborne scent to be effective at that distance. After years of relying upon airborne scent trails, my guess is that under normal conditions a buck might be able to pick up the scent and follow it in from a distance of 100 yards or less. I look upon airborne scent trails as a short-range complement to my long-range ground trails, as well as a secondary cover scent for my own human odor.

Like most hunters that have been using scents for a long time, the first scent bombs or scent canisters I used were homemade. Al-

Everything you need to make a mock scrape.

though today I rely upon the highly absorbent scent wicks, the old 35mm film canister filled with clean cotton still does a great job and the price is right. Just fill a clean canister with cotton. When you get to your stand, pluck some of the cotton up to form a wick and add a liquid doe-in-estrous lure. Use a clothespin to attach the canister to a branch or bush two to four feet off the ground. This height is important; higher and the scent will likely go right over a buck's nose, lower and the scent has a tendency to hug the ground.

I've seen some mighty fancy diagrams instructing where to place scent canisters, but I don't get too scientific. Just put four to eight canisters in a circle around your stand (see illustration below). That way you cover all of the bases no matter what the fickle breeze does during the day. One important point is to be sure to hang each canister where you can get a shot if a buck has his nose to the scent. Not only are airborne scents good for bringing bucks into range, they are excellent at holding a buck's attention while you draw and

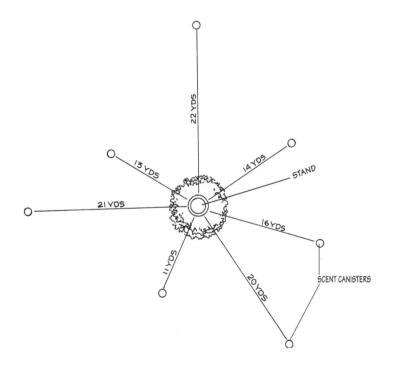

make the shot. In fact, I know of two Boone & Crockett bucks taken by archers just across the river from my home that would not have been killed had the bucks not taken the time to investigate a well-placed scent canister.

Key points to remember:
- Always wear rubber gloves when handling scent applicators.
- Scent canisters or wicks double nicely as yardage markers.

MEMORY SCENT TRAILS

We all know that deer, and big bucks in particular, are most active at night. For instance, research indicates that a buck will make 80 percent of its scrapes under the cover of darkness. All of this nighttime movement is bad news for hunters. While I cannot do anything about a buck's penchant for nighttime activities, I can encourage a buck to visit my stand site during the day through what I refer to as memory scent trails. Here is the deal. Make a mock scrape or doctor a real scrape within range of your stand. Put some tarsal gland buck lure in the scrape and a generous dose of doe-in-estrous urine. Use an old trick and punch a few holes in the lid of a jar (baby food jars work well) of scent and bury the jar in a real or mock scrape, or bury an H.S. Buc-n-Rut Scent Wafer in the scrape. Either option will keep the scrape fresh for days in your absence. Be sure to put some buck scent on the overhanging branch. Make a couple of false rubs nearby and apply a little buck scent to each rub. Now when a buck comes through at night you can bet that he will notice the rubs and scrapes. Odds are he may add his own scent to the scrape and work over your mock rubs. The buck will remember where he smelled those tantalizing odors. The next day, maybe on his way back to his bed in the pink light of dawn, he might make a little sidetrip to check things out. Or maybe he will remember your doctored rubs and scrapes as he lies restlessly in his bed that day. The memory may just put him on his feet a little earlier than normal and then in your sights.

Key points to remember:

- Memory trails employing scrapes are most effective during the scraping period of the rut (the two weeks prior to the first wave of does entering estrous) and during the early part of the breeding phase of the rut. Fake rubs can be effective earlier in the season.
- The overhanging branch is more important than the scrape itself, so be sure to doctor the branch with a buck scent that contains glandular secretions from the preorbital, forehead, tarsal, or nasal glands.
- Since the first serious scrapes are usually made by the dominant buck in an area, try to beat him to the punch by a couple of days. That will get his attention!

15

CONTROLLING HUMAN ODOR

Four of us were bowhunting deer on Montana's famed Milk River. We were attempting to get some footage for the Realtree television show and Monster Bucks video series, so each of us had a cameraman. The whitetail deer that call the Milk River home are not difficult to figure out. They bed in the willow thickets along the river banks by day and then in late afternoon begin filtering out into adjacent alfalfa fields to feed. In the morning the process reverses itself. It's a fun place to hunt because you always see lots of deer and some of them are very nice bucks.

My cameraman was a young man by the name of Mark Womack, a senior at Auburn University in Georgia, who was fortunate enough to be working for Realtree as part of his internship. (What a gig for a young man who enjoys the outdoors and loves to hunt.) Mark and I hit it off right away and before we headed out for the first evening on stand, I asked Mark if he would mind following an odor control plan. Mark was game, so I made some suggestions as far as showering before the hunt and keeping clothes clean and then gave him one of my extra Scent-Lok suits to wear. It was September, and the weather was warm as it usually is in the West at this time of the year. Even the lightest Scent-Lok suit is warmer than the lightest weight camouflage clothing without the activated-charcoal liner, but Mark never complained.

A lot of hunters are convinced that the only way to go undetected by a whitetail's sense of smell is to make sure that the deer never get downwind of their position. That's a great theory, but I've never seen evidence of it working very well. It sure does not work on the Milk River, as in the evenings you hunt from stands where the breeze is blowing from the willow thicket bedding areas into the fields. This way the deer cannot smell you as they make their way from the thick bedding areas to the lush alfalfa fields. But once in

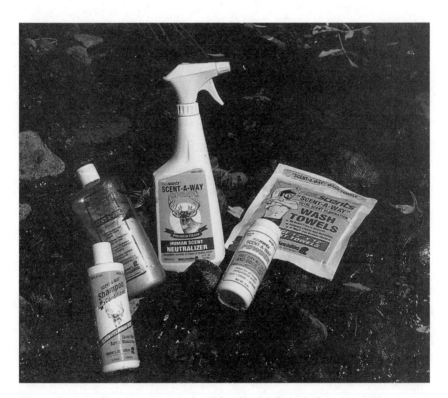

These odor control products are not gimmicks; they really work if used correctly.

the field in front of your stand, then what? You guessed it. If the buck you are looking for happens to be one of the first deer past your stand, you are in business. Usually, though, the larger bucks come into the field after the does, fawns, and smaller bucks. Do you think a big buck is going to walk into an alfalfa field where he has just listened to deer snorting and blowing because they have gotten your scent? Do you think Mr. Big is dumb enough to amble out into a field after all the other deer have vacated because they got a snoot full of human odor? Not hardly.

Odor control is important anytime you are hunting whitetail deer, but it is especially important when you hunt an area that has a lot of deer. The more deer there are, the better the odds that some of those deer are going to get downwind of your position. It's a matter of mathematics and there is not much you can do about it.

What you can do is control your human odor to the extent that the deer that do get downwind of your position either do not smell you at all or pick up only a hint of human odor and, because it is so weak, determine that it does not represent any danger to them. Either way, you win.

Mark and I were the only hunter and cameraman team to be taking full precaution with controlling our human odor that week. Around the sagging supper table Donna set for us each evening we would share the events of the day and invariably each of the other teams would report that they had "cleared a field" when deer got their scent. Mark and I hunted together for seven days and never cleared a field, which means that when one deer gets your scent and sounds the alarm, all of the deer vacate the alfalfa field. Not what you want to see. In fact, even though I would venture a guess that we probably had well over 100 deer downwind of our position at one time or another during that week, we never did spook any of them.

When I finally did kill a buck, it was from a hay bale ground blind, and Mark shot footage of several deer, including a pretty darn nice nine-point buck actually eating hay off of my blind while I was inside. At one time, the buck was so close to me that I could have easily grabbed him by his antlers. If any of those deer had gotten either my scent or Mark's scent and spooked, odds are good that the buck that I killed later that evening would never have come out into the field or near that blind.

By the time that week was over, three hunters and three cameramen were busy re-evaluating their position on controlling human odor.

Don't get me wrong, I'm not saying that it is possible to become 100 percent odor free. You are not going to escape detection by all of the deer that get downwind of your stand. However, with strict adherence to an odor control program, you can greatly reduce the amount of human odor that drifts downwind. Doing this will result in your being scented less frequently and will add up to more opportunities to not only see deer, but to have better shooting opportunities at the deer you do see.

How important is human odor control in my overall hunting plan? In the past 30 years, two decisions have contributed more to whatever success I have enjoyed as a deer hunter than all others. Those two decisions were to hunt from a treestand as often as possible and to get serious about controlling human odor.

I am amazed at the number of hunters today who not only do nothing to control their odor, but scoff at the whole idea of odor control. We live in a nation that now puts men and women into space with such regularity that it is no longer headline news. Our chemists, biologists, and doctors have found cures and vaccines for some of the world's deadliest diseases. Why is it so difficult to believe that we have at our disposal products which inhibit human odor?

A whitetail deer's sense of smell is his number one defensive mechanism. Granted, a whitetail has good vision, especially when it comes to detecting motion, and those big ears enable a whitetail to not only hear very well, but to pinpoint the origin of the sounds that it hears. Without that incredible sense of smell, though, it is likely that the whitetail deer would have been extinct by now. A whitetail may question what it sees, it may want to further confirm what it hears, but when a whitetail detects danger with its sense of smell the confirming process has ceased. A whitetail, you might say, lives or dies by its nose.

I was about to say that it was probably sometime in the mid-1980s that I began to get serious about trying to minimize the amount of human odor I spread around each time I went deer hunting, but looking back, I can see that I was into odor control long before that. For years, I hung my hunting clothes outside where they could freshen in the air. Later, I started storing my outerwear with leaves, dirt, or pine needles, letting the fabric absorb the smells of the earth. I suppose I've used about every cover scent ever invented at one time or another. I doubt that I will ever forget the look on the

I spray down everything with an odor neutralizer.

faces of the other folks in the restaurant the time I stopped for a bite on the way home from hunting one evening and forgot about the essence of skunk I had liberally poured on my boots. It was sometime in the '80s, though, that I began to use odor-reducing sprays and powders. When Scent-Lok introduced that first green suit with something they called activated charcoal in 1990, I was one of the first hunters to be wearing one.

There have been plenty of gimmicks and rip-offs in the odor control arena. There are in any consumer category. But the products that actually do what they are supposed to do survive and find acceptance with hunters. Today, we have a wide array of products available to help us minimize human odor. I cannot imagine why any serious whitetail hunter would not take advantage of this technology.

Here are the steps I suggest you take if you want to dramatically reduce the number of times each season deer detect you with that undeniably incredible sense of smell:

1) Shower with a scent-free soap and shampoo before each hunt whenever possible. If you cannot shower use Scent-A-Way wash towels.

2) Use a scent-free anti-perspirant. If you use a powder make sure it is unscented.

3) Dress in clothing that has been washed in an odor-free laundry soap and stored in a scent-safe bag or air-tight container. This should include underwear and socks.

4) Sprinkle an odor-eliminating powder in your boots and rub some in the sweat band of your cap.

5) Wear an activated-charcoal suit, including the hood or face mask. I know that the hoods are uncomfortable, that they sometimes interfere with peripheral vision and with your ability to hear (I cut ear slots in mine), but I've proven to myself many times that if I do not wear the hood, the effectiveness of

the suit is cut in half. I try to put on my Scent-Lok suit after I arrive at my destination. If I have a long hike into my stand, I often carry it in with me and stop about 100 yards before I get to my stand to put it on.

6) Spray down your outer layer of clothing and all of your gear with an odor-eliminating spray before getting into your stand and repeat every few hours while on stand.

GETTING THE MOST OUT OF YOUR SCENT-LOK SUIT

Hunting clothing with activated charcoal for controlling human odor is a major investment for most of us. Whether you purchase the original Scent-Lok garments, clothing made with W.L. Gore's Supprescent, or an outfit featuring Scent-Tek from Robinson Labs, you can figure on paying anywhere from $150 up to $500 for a complete set of activated-charcoal clothing. Take care of your activated-charcoal garments and they will serve you well for many years.

I've been wearing activated-charcoal garments while hunting whitetail deer and other big game since 1991, the year after Scent-Lok first introduced their original green liner to the hunting world. Since then, I've averaged 75 days each season wearing this clothing. This does not make me an expert on activated charcoal, but it has provided me with some in-the-field experience. But before we get into how you can make sure that your garments are doing the job for you every time you put them on and how you can wring the most mileage possible out of your activated-charcoal clothing, it is important to understand how activated charcoal works to help control human odor.

A layer of activated charcoal, the best of which is made from coconut hulls, is sandwiched between two layers of fabric. Just as the filter on your furnace captures and holds dust and debris that otherwise would be spread around your home, activated charcoal, through a process called *adsorption*, traps and holds the scent molecules that make you and I stink to whitetail deer and other critters with equally sensitive noses. This process is no gimmick. Activated charcoal has been used in many industrial applications and by the military for many years. Greg Sesselmann and George Schrink, a couple of engineers with expertise in the aerospace carbon filtration field, founded Scent-Lok in the early '90s because they envisioned an application for activated charcoal technology in the hunting world. The rest, as they say, is history.

Look at activated charcoal under a microscope and you will see that each particle is a maze of nooks, crannies, and crevices. It is within these nooks and crannies that the gunk which makes you and I stink is trapped and held so that it cannot reach the atmosphere. Naturally, once the nooks and crannies are full, the activated charcoal can no longer do its job. To "cleanse" the activated charcoal you reactivate it with heat. Heat causes the activated charcoal to purge itself. The problem here is that it takes at least 800 degrees for complete reactivation, a temperature you cannot attain without burning up the suit itself. However, you can attain a degree of reactivation that will render the activated charcoal serviceable once again by putting the suit into a clothes dryer on its hottest setting for 45 minutes. Before placing my suit in a dryer, I always spray down the interior of the dryer with an odor eliminator to kill any foreign odors.

When I take my suit out of the dryer I roll it up tightly and place it in a Scent Safe clothing bag from H.S. Scents. Do not use a standard garbage bag. The plastic used in garbage bags has a distinctive odor and this odor will be transferred to your clothing. The Scent Safe bag goes inside one of those green Scent Safe travel bags. This double protection insures that my activated-charcoal garments will not be subjected to any foreign odors prior to the hunt.

I usually drive to my hunting area wearing an old pair of sweats and dress in my activated-charcoal garments on the tailgate of my truck after I arrive. This insures that I will not contaminate my clothing with odors from the house or camp, on any stops along the way for food or fuel, or with odors from the vehicle itself. The most common mistake I see hunters make when it comes to activated-charcoal clothing is getting dressed at home or in camp and then driving to the hunting area. After I am done hunting for the day, my activated-charcoal garments come off when I get back to my vehicle and are stored in the odor-free double bag system again. This dressing and undressing at the vehicle is admittedly a hassle, but it is worth the effort.

One of the questions I am most frequently asked regarding activated-charcoal garments is how often should they be reacti-

My clothing stays in a Scent Safe bag until I am ready to get dressed. If it is not too warm I dress at the pickup and then hike into the stand. Otherwise, I will carry my clothing nearly to the stand and then stop and get dressed.

vated? Unfortunately, there is no pat answer to that question because there are too many variables to be considered. One variable is that each of us is an individual when it comes to how much odor we give off. Put simply, some of us stink more than others. Naturally, if you are one of those who is on the high end of the stink spectrum, you will need to reactivate more often than someone on the low end. The second variable that must be considered is the weather. In warm weather we tend to sweat and stink more than we do in cold weather. Third, the activated-charcoal garments themselves must be taken into account. There are dozens of choices out there. Garments designed for warm weather sometimes have less activated charcoal sandwiched between the two layers of fabric than do garments designed for hunting in colder weather. The less activated charcoal you have working for you, the more often you will need to reactivate. My advice is, when in doubt, reactivate. You cannot "wear out" the activated charcoal by frequent reactivation. I throw mine in the dryer after about every 30 hours of hunting.

Washing your activated-charcoal garments does little to increase the effectiveness of the activated charcoal. I wash mine only when the exterior of the garment has become covered with mud or grime, or if I suspect that the garment has been contaminated by a foreign odor, such as gasoline, diesel fuel, or vehicle exhaust. When you do wash your activated-charcoal garments, use a soap that does not leave behind any odor or soap residue, such as Atsko Sport-Wash.

If you care for your activated-charcoal garments, they will do their job for you for a long, long time.

NOT JUST FOR BOWHUNTERS

Although bowhunters were the first to embrace activated-charcoal clothing and still account for the bulk of sales, those who hunt deer with firearms are slowly beginning to realize that controlling their human odor will lead to seeing more deer and having better shots at close range deer. It is the most important step they can take to improving their odds of drawing a bead on a real bruiser of a buck.

I do a lot of deer hunting with a muzzleloader, and I cannot remember the last time in the last ten years that I entered the woods carrying my smokepole without a layer of activated charcoal between my hide and the whitetail's nose. Those who hunt with shotguns and slugs also need deer to be reasonably close for a clean kill and will benefit greatly from using activated charcoal. But I believe that even those who hunt with centerfire rifles, which in the hands of a competent rifleman are deadly at long range, can benefit from activated charcoal technology. Most of the deer killed in North America, regardless of the type of firearm used, are taken at well under 100 yards.

Every deer hunter with a few seasons under his or her belt has experienced the frustration of having a deer blowing and snorting in alarm as it picked up the hunter's scent. For every deer we see spook or hear snort, there are probably two or three others that simply detect our presence with their sense of smell and take evasive action to avoid us. Wearing an activated-charcoal suit will dramatically decrease these instances.

16

FINE TUNE YOUR TREESTANDS

Based on my own experiences and those of other seasoned hunters, I'm convinced that often the difference between a shot and no shot, or a good shot and a poor shot, or just seeing deer versus having opportunities at deer, is made by the little things we will talk about in this chapter. You might call it fine tuning; I often call it "tweaking" (as in to take something good and make it better). Whatever you want to call it, these are the little things that often make or break a hunt.

An incident from last season reminds me of just how seemingly insignificant some of these changes can be, and yet how dramatic the results. On a farm I hunt a couple of hours from my home, I had, after a thorough scouting job, hung three fixed-position stands in what I felt were the three best locations on the 160 acres. My number one spot was overlooking a location where a five-strand barbed-wire fence sagged from previous damage, creating the perfect crossing spot for deer. Deer meandering down from the high ridges, where they prefer to bed, would cross the fence on their way to feed on the abundant acorns on the little oak flat where my stand was situated and later mosey out to dine on soybeans, corn, and al-falfa. I hung the stand 20 feet up a ramrod-straight basswood tree, just 15 steps from the fence crossing. Because I prefer to shoot sitting down whenever possible, I hung the stand so that the fence crossing was off my left shoulder, the perfect angle for a right-handed shooter. I felt confident that everything was perfect and could not wait to hunt the stand.

But on the first evening, I quickly realized that everything was not perfect. The first deer to come along was a lone button buck that hopped over the fence and turned broadside to follow the heavily-used trail, just as I had envisioned. But the second deer was a different story. It was a long-necked, hump-nosed, mature doe with a pair of fawns in tow. Big bucks get all of the credit for being the "smartest" deer, but they don't hold a candle to a mature doe. Does are entrusted with the job of raising the next generation, so nature has instilled in them an incredible wariness. The doe came down the ridge and then stopped in a small opening about 50 yards away and stared holes right through me. Because the ridge dropped off steeply, the doe and I were on the same level, despite that fact that I was 20 feet up a tree. I was dressed in camouflage, including a full face mask and gloves, and I had not moved, but that old doe knew that the blob in the tree had not been there the last time she used that trail, and for an old doe that is all it takes, just something out of place. The old gal stared for a long time and I was afraid she was going to go into one of those snorting and blowing sessions for which the old biddies are so famous, but she did not; nor did she continue down the trail to the fence crossing. Instead, she took her twins in a wide loop around my stand. I hoped that it was just a fluke that the old doe had nailed me and continued my vigil.

The next deer to use the same trail, another doe, this one with a single fawn, convinced me in a hurry that the first encounter had not been a fluke. Just like the first doe, when she reached the opening on the steep ridge she stopped and stared right at me. Eventually, she too worked her way around me, well out of bow range.

It was prime time by now, the sun just about gone behind the ridge, and I did not want to move, but I knew that I had to do something. I stepped off the stand, loosened the strap, and swung the stand around to the backside of the tree. Then I screwed in another step to allow me to step onto the platform easily and climbed aboard. The whole operation might have taken five minutes.

Preparing stand sites is faster with two people. While seated in the stand, it is easy to point out to a partner on the ground which branches need to be trimmed.

Now my stand was facing directly away from where the deer approached. Not ideal for sitting comfortably and being able to scan the area where you expect deer to come from, but even a fussy old nag of a doe can't see *through* a basswood tree!

I hunted that stand a half-dozen times last season and saw deer each time. The only deer that ever showed any sign of nervousness when approaching that fence crossing were those two does that had picked me off that first evening. Old does, being female, of course, *never* forget!

TOO MUCH EMPHASIS ON COMFORT

I am convinced that most bowhunters put too much emphasis on comfort when selecting stand sites. Let's look again at that fence-crossing stand. When I put that stand up I knew that the basswood in which I hung the stand offered no cover in the way of branches and that was a concern. However, I convinced myself that if I sat still, no deer would spot me. The key word here is *sat*. As I said earlier, I prefer to shoot sitting down. I also prefer to remain seated most of the time while I am on stand, and I like to be comfortable. I want a tree that is either straight or leans slightly away from me, so that I can lean back and be comfortable. I want to be able to easily scan the direction from which I think deer will be approaching without craning my neck or making other contortions. And I don't want a knot or a sawed-off branch stub sticking me in a shoulder blade when I'm trying to stay comfortable in my stand. There is nothing wrong with any of this, of course, unless you pick your trees and the position for your stand based upon comfort rather than maximum effectiveness. For maximum effectiveness, my stand in that basswood tree had to be placed on the backside where it was facing away from the direction the deer took. This meant that instead of sitting on the comfortable net seat, I had to stand the whole time while peeking around the tree—not nearly as comfortable, but ten times as deadly.

One of the best bowhunters in the country, Stan Potts of Illinois, hangs most of his stands on the backside of the tree. It's no fun standing for hours facing the tree, peering around the sides to watch for approaching deer, but as Stan puts it, "By golly, a big buck can do a lot of amazing things, but I never found one yet that could see right through two foot of solid oak." Not that Stan always hangs his stands that way. If the tree has plenty of leaf cover, there is no need to hunt from the back, but late in the season, when leaf cover is down, you will almost always find Stan hugging the backside.

Speaking of comfort, I'm reminded of my good friend Tom Indrebo, who runs Bluff Country Outfitters. Tom hangs around 60 portable stands each season, and nobody I know spends more time finding the exact tree for the stand and the precise position to hang the stand. The man is a perfectionist when it comes to hanging stands and it drives me crazy to go along with him. He takes into consideration where the deer are most likely to come from, which wind directions will work for that particular stand, how the hunter can access the stand without leaving scent on the ground or tromping through bedding areas, what kind of concealment the stand offers in terms of branches or other trees in the background, and a dozen other important considerations. Comfort, I don't believe, is a consideration. Some of Tom's stands were absolute torture chambers to sit in, but I have never hunted out of one that was not in exactly the right tree and in exactly the right position in that tree to afford the best shot.

DON'T BE TOO QUICK TO MOVE YOUR STAND

Here is one I've been guilty of on more occasions than I care to admit. In fact, I did it again just last October. I was bowhunting a farm just minutes north of my home in southeastern Minnesota. Before the season began I had hung several stands on the farm, my favorite being one that occupied a corner of the largest block of timber. An overgrown tangle of fenceline, a natural travel route, intersected with the corner of the woods. The farmer who worked the land had cut a ten-yard-wide swath through the fenceline right where it joined the woods so that he could easily move machinery from one field to another. Deer moved through this opening with regularity. One deer in particular was in the habit of crossing there, a dandy ten-point buck that I had watched throughout late summer as he fattened on soybeans and alfalfa. After a fresh rain one evening, I walked out to where the buck had been feeding in a soybean field and got a good look at his track so that I could recognize it when I saw it again. Like the track of most mature bucks, this one was blunt instead of pointed and a solid three inches across. I found that track often in the soft soil of the cut through the fenceline.

The first evening I hunted that stand, the big ten point did not make his way down the fenceline. Instead, right at dusk, I spotted him across the field from my stand where a blunt finger of timber jutted up from the river and into the field. He worked a couple of overhanging branches and was still along that edge when darkness enveloped him. The next morning, I hung a stand along the edge where the buck had worked the overhanging branches (no scrapes, just licking branches) the evening before.

Again, right at dusk, the time of day when the big boys are finally comfortable moving around, the ten pointer sauntered right through that gap in the fenceline and right under my vacant stand. Frustrated, I snatched my Tru-Talker from inside my jacket and sent a series of tending grunts floating across the bean stubble. The buck heard the grunts and came sauntering slowly across the field. With the light fading quickly, I willed the buck to hurry. He finally made his way across the light-colored stubble and stepped into the timber just 60 yards from where I perched, but as soon as he entered the woods I lost him. It was too dark. I kept track of him through the sound of his steps in the fallen leaves and knew that he was moving my way, searching, no doubt, for the buck he had heard grunting.

When he was only ten yards away I finally saw the white of his throat patch as he lifted his head to sniff one of the scent wicks I had hung around my stand. It was too late to shoot. The buck hung around for five, maybe ten minutes and then I heard him walk off. I don't know if the buck detected something amiss and avoided that place the rest of the season or if perhaps he was taken by another hunter or hit by a car. Whatever the case, I never saw him again. If I had followed my own rule, which is to never move a stand on the basis of one sighting but to wait for a second to confirm the first, I would have had my opportunity at that buck.

This is obviously a well-traveled deer trail, but don't be too hasty about putting up a stand. First check off to either side of the main trail for a smaller, less noticeable parallel trail. If you find one, that is where a big buck is likely to travel.

Another outfitter friend, Mike Pavlick, runs his Golden Triangle Whitetail operation on several thousand acres of prime whitetail habitat in western Illinois. Mike is a standaholic. All summer and all winter he is scouting for new places to hang stands and putting stands up for the bowhunters who hunt with him in the fall. Before a stand ever goes up, Mike is pretty darn sure that the location he has chosen is the very best for that situation.

"But invariably," says Mike, "one of my hunters will come in from hunting, foaming at the mouth over the big buck he has seen just out of range. Of course, these hunters want me to move the stand to where they saw the big buck. I try to convince them to give the original stand another try and then if they happen to see the same buck or a different buck using the same travel route as the first, I will move the stand for them. Most go ahead with this plan and very often they end up killing a good buck from the stand I originally hung. But sometimes a guest is emphatic that the stand has to be moved, so I go ahead and move it. I can only recall one hunter who had a shot at a buck after I moved a stand for him, but I've lost count of the hunters who have come back in with a long look on their face to report that a good buck walked right past the original stand.

"Sometimes moving the stand just a few yards can make a difference, but most of the time, if there was some thought put into hanging the stand in the first place, you are better off hunting from that location."

A CASE FOR CLIMBERS

When it comes to quick adjustments in the woods, you can't beat a climbing stand.

Want to hunt the opposite side of the tree? No problem with a climber, just "walk" the stand around to the other side. It's maybe a one-minute operation. Need to go higher or lower to take advantage of background cover or for a better view? No problem.

Or let's say a couple of deer pass by on the same trail just out of range of your present location. With a climber, you are talking one minute to climb down, another to walk over to the new tree, two more minutes to climb the tree and cinch down the stand—in five minutes or so you are in position. Try that with a fixed-position or ladder stand.

THE ALL-IMPORTANT ENTRY AND EXIT

When selecting stand locations it is important that you be able to get into the stand without alerting the deer you are planning to hunt. This sounds elementary, but I cannot tell you how often I have seen hunters march right through the bedding area on their way to an evening stand or through the places deer are feeding on their hike to the morning stands. Then they wonder why they don't see any deer. It's simple: If you spook the deer you plan to hunt before you get into your stand, the odds of that deer coming along and posing beneath your stand are about as good as your viewing a total eclipse of the sun.

I'll never forget the time I was invited to hunt with a bowhunter in western Illinois who had quite a reputation for taking nice bucks. The first morning we parked the truck along a muddy field road, walked a short distance down the two-track, and then cut across a harvested cornfield. Deer scattered out of that field like a covey of quail. My host did not even break stride and I assumed that he had somehow not heard the noise the deer had made exiting the field. I quickly caught up to him and grabbed him by an arm. Startled, he stopped, turned to me, and whispered, "What's the matter?"

"This field was full of deer," I whispered back.

"Sure. It always is," he replied and started walking again.

After an uneventful morning on stand not far from the other end of the picked cornfield, I hiked back out and met my host at the pickup for a little lunch and midday break. Without being critical, I brought up the number of deer I had heard run out of the field that morning and how it was sure too bad that we could not find another route into our morning stands so that we would not have to blow the deer out of the field.

"Oh, we could park up on the main road, cut across that pasture up on top, and then drop down into the woods and get to the stands that way," my host offered. "Of course, you have to walk about twice as far. This is the easiest way."

The "easiest way," I think, is where most of us get into trouble. Very often, the easiest way is not the best way to enter or exit a stand. When I find a potentially good stand location, I ask myself if I am going to be able to get to the stand in the morning or the evening without disturbing the deer. Then I ask myself if I can get out of the stand and back to my vehicle without walking through the deer that I am depending upon to make that stand a good place to sit. If, after exploring all of the options, the answer is no to either question, I write that potential stand location off and go look for another one.

This does not mean that you can avoid spooking the occasional deer going to or from your stand. This cannot be helped. I'm talking about things that can be helped, like purposefully walking right through a bedding area on the way into an evening stand site or through a field full of feeding deer as you approach your morning stand. Or, nearly as bad, walking by on the upwind end of these places. The fewer deer you disturb in getting to your stand the better.

Never overlook water as an option. If you can wade up a shallow creek and then slip right into a tree on the bank, I would consider this the perfect entrance. Even a whitetail cannot smell your scent in water. I've used my canoe to reach several stands along deeper creeks and small rivers and have poled a small duckboat across a shallow cattail marsh to reach my stand on a little willow island. It does not occur often, but if you find a set-up that allows you to enter and exit the stand by water instead of land, take advantage of the situation.

Most hunters do not worry too much about exiting the stand. That's a mistake, especially if you plan to hunt that stand again. If you make every effort not to disturb deer as you exit your stand and hike back to your vehicle it will pay dividends.

I've had many hunters tell me that it does no harm to walk right through feeding deer in the dark, whether on the way to the stand in the morning or returning to the vehicle in the evenings, because deer just scatter as you walk through them and then go right back to feeding minutes after you are out of sight. To some extent, I will admit that this is true. Blow the deer out of a field once, and they probably will not change their feeding patterns. But let it happen a second or third time and I guarantee you the deer will either go somewhere else to feed, or they will plan to do their dining when you are not around. Mature deer are the most likely to change their patterns with the least influence from you.

TO TRIM OR NOT TO TRIM

When it comes to trimming the tree in which you hang your stand and pruning shooting lanes, I know this much: If you get six different bowhunters discussing the subject, there are going to be six different opinions on how much to trim or prune. Me, I don't argue with anyone. If what you are doing is working for you, stick with it. If it is not, then read on.

I do as little trimming in the tree as possible. My theory here is simple: the more branches I trim, the better the odds that a deer is going to spot me. The days when deer did not look up are over in most parts of the country, so you have to be more careful with trimming than you did 20 or even 10 years ago.

It is easy to go crazy with the trimming if you hang your stands when there are leaves still on the branches. Try to look at the tree as if it were naked. This will give you a feel for what really needs to be trimmed.

Many hunters end up trimming more from the tree than neces-sary because they are not properly equipped for the job. Let's say you have a branch that juts out from the tree just above your right shoul-der as you are seated in the stand. You would like to leave the branch because not only does it help provide good cover, but with the addition of a few hangers it will make a great place to hang your rattling horns, binoculars, and grunt call. The branch will also pro-vide great stability when standing, since you can lean against it and take some of the pressure off your legs. The problem is that it ex-tends well out from the trunk of the tree and the drooping, bushy

A telescoping saw pole allows you to reach branches that might deflect your arrow.

outer portions obscure your view and make it impossible to shoot to a good trail. A good telescoping saw takes care of this problem. With a telescoping saw you can reach out either from up in your stand or while standing on the ground and trim away only the portions of the branch that are going to interfere with your shot while retaining the rest of the branch.

How important is a telescoping saw? If I hang 50 stands each season, I will use the telescoping saw on at least 40 of them. I don't know a single serious bowhunter who does not own and use one.

When it comes to shooting lanes, my favorite stands are those where I don't have to snip a single twig or bush. The less I can disturb the immediate area, the better I like it. Unfortunately, the best stand sites rarely offer such convenience. Mature deer of either sex do not miss much that goes on in their home area. Cut a sapling and leave that gleaming, white stub above the ground and you can bet that the next time through, a mature buck or doe will take notice of it. That is why most hunters try to cut them off flush to the ground. Even then, a mature deer tends to notice when there is a new opening created, no matter how inconspicuous you try to make it. That is why, whenever possible, I try to cut my shooting lanes well before the season. If there is not too much snow on the ground, my favorite time to trim shooting lanes is during the month or two after the last deer season closes. If snow cover is heavy, I wait for spring melt and then get it done before the woods green up. This gives the deer plenty of time to become accustomed to the new trimming. My most painful example of how aware a mature deer is of everything that goes on in its home area took place a few years ago several miles from my home. It was the day before the Minnesota firearms opener. Minnesota is one of the few states that holds its firearms deer season during the rut, so I headed for the woods that afternoon with my heavy set of rattling antlers slung over one shoulder and a portable stand over the other. I hung the stand at the corner of the largest chunk of timber where a brushy fencerow intersected with the corner of the timber. I knew that deer often used that fencerow when traveling between the mostly small, scattered parcels of timber in the area. I did as little trimming as possible, but I did have to take down a small aspen tree, about as big around as my arm, that was directly in line with the edge of the picked cornfield 30 yards from my stand. I only had a small hand saw with me, so instead of cutting the tree off at ground level as I usually do when using a larger saw, I opted to cut it off at about waist height where it was not so thick. About halfway through my cut, the heavy top of the tree caused it to buckle and instead of a clean cut, the trunk split lengthwise. I should have taken the time to make another cut, but I did not. I simply pulled the tree down so that it lay on top of the brush and hastily climbed into my stand.

An hour later I rattled up the biggest buck that has ever come to my horns in Minnesota. As so often happens, this buck did not come from where I had anticipated the action. He instead came out of a CRP field on the far side of the picked cornfield. I suspect that after a night of carousing the big buck had bedded in the CRP field. When I saw him he was halfway across that chopped cornfield and coming hard. I dropped the horns, grabbed my bow, slapped my release on the string, and got ready. The buck was 20 yards from the edge of the woods and 50 yards from my stand when he suddenly slammed on the brakes and went to full attention, staring hard into the woods. I could not figure out what had gone wrong. The wind was not perfect, but it was not bad. Despite my excitement and anticipation, I knew I had not moved. I thought maybe there was another deer in the woods that had gotten his attention. But it wasn't another deer at all. It was that split popple tree. The buck, even though he had something on his mind when he came to my horns, instantly recognized that the split tree was something different. Of course, he had no way of knowing that I had caused the little tree to split. It could just as easily have been the wind or a brush with farm machinery. But it did not matter to the buck. The fact was that the split tree did not belong, it was something different, something out of place, and it made the buck nervous. Instead of coming straight on in like I am sure he would have had he not seen the raw inner wood of that sapling, the buck went cautious on me. He cut into the woods, and without ever getting close enough to give me a shot, he circled my stand. I knew what he was doing and I could not do a darn thing about it. I had taken all of the precautions with my scent that I always do, but it was not enough. The buck got straight down-breeze and stood there for three or four minutes with his nose high, trying to get a fix on what I suspect was just a thread of human odor drifting his way. Finally, he just walked away.

I know that many hunters do not believe that a little thing like a branch stub that wasn't there yesterday can be enough to put a mature deer on the alert. The reason they have trouble believing is that most of the time we do not see the deer's initial reaction to our pruning efforts. Deer move much more at night than they do during the day, and it is more likely that a deer will make that initial discovery sometime during the night. You can bet he will be curious about the snipped branches and the paths you have created. He will likely walk each shooting lane and sniff every branch and bush. No matter how careful you were to wear rubber boots and gloves, odds are he will detect your scent here and there. A mature deer will simply avoid that place for awhile. He is not really spooked, just cautious. If the shooting lanes are made weeks or, better yet, months before the season opens, there is an excellent chance that the buck will fully accept the shooting lanes as just part of the scheme of things by the time the season opens. I always figure that if I hang a stand and trim shooting lanes during the season my best chance to kill that buck is going to be on his first visit, the one where he does his initial inspection of my handiwork.

17

ALL-DAY SITS ON STAND

D o you know why you see so little written in the outdoor magazines about sitting in a stand all day? The editors of those magazines figure few readers want to read about deer hunting's version of a colonoscopy. Don't ever kid yourself, there is nothing fun about sitting on a deer stand from dark to dark, and the average deer hunter is just not going to do it. But I have a hunch that if you have read this far you might be a little different from the average deer hunter.

From my observations, it appears that deer hunters can be divided into three categories. Category one deer hunters are very casual about the sport. In fact, if not for the camaraderie of family and friends, category one hunters would probably not bother hunting deer at all. They do not even entertain the thought of an all-day sit and look strangely upon those of us who do.

Category two deer hunters are more on the serious side. These hunters watch a deer hunting video now and then, read a few magazine articles on the subject, try to get out and scout before the season, sight in their guns or bows, and practice with them. Category two deer hunters talk about sitting on stand all day, try to sit on stand all day, but rarely do. Most of this nation's seven million deer hunters fit into this category.

Category three deer hunters have slipped over the edge. If one of these hunters from upstate New York draws a deer tag for southern Iowa, guess where the family will spend its summer vacation? "Oh, don't worry honey, Centerville, Iowa, is beautiful this time of year, you and the kids are going to love it." Speaking of scouting, this is not something a category three hunter rushes out to do a day or two before the season. Scouting, either on foot, in a plane, on the Internet, or on the phone with another over-the-edge hunter, is what consumes all of the days he is not actually hunting. Category three hunters aren't much on camaraderie; in fact, most of them are loners. Most of these whitetail addicts work like driven dogs ten or eleven months of the year and then take a month or two off, with or without pay, to get their fix in the whitetail woods. Category three hunters tend to kill big bucks with amazing consistency. Category three hunters are veterans of the all-day sit.

There are few guarantees in the wacky world of whitetail hunting, but I will guarantee you that if you get in the habit of sitting on stand all day in a good location, under the right conditions, you will see more deer than you ever have before. The law of averages dictates that some of those deer will be wearing headgear. Once or twice a season, a real bruiser might even cruise by.

Right conditions and good location are the keys here. Unless both are in your favor you are wasting your time subjecting yourself to the torture of an all-day sit. Did I say torture? Wait a minute, isn't deer hunting supposed to be fun? What happened to all of that stuff about glorious sunrises, scampering squirrels, twittering birds, and even more glorious sunsets? Oh, you will see all of that and more on an all-day sit, but trust me on this one, after awhile, boredom, fatigue, stiff muscles, complaining joints, self doubt, and the cold will turn your day of communing with nature into a furious test of will-power. After having subjected myself to more all-day sits than a mature human being should admit to, I have come up with some tricks for dealing with all of these culprits.

The truth about midday deer hunting is that for most of the season it is a waste of time. This has to do with the whitetail's daily movement patterns. Deer feed heaviest in the evening, continue to munch off and on during the night, grab a bite as day breaks, and slip into bedding cover during the first hour or so of the new day. Sometime in late morning or early afternoon, most deer will get up out of their beds, relieve themselves, browse a bit, and then lie back down for the rest of the afternoon. This kind of daily pattern dictates that the most deer movement can be expected early and late in the day as deer trade back and forth between the food source and the bedding area, which is why most hunters hunt

It takes commitment and patience to sit it out all day, but under the right conditions, it is your best bet for taking a nice buck.

mornings, evenings, or both, but rarely midday. That's a good plan for most of the season.

There are three situations, however, that can make midday hunting pay off big time: hunting pressure, the rut, and what I term late-season food stress. When any of these three factors comes into play, midday hunting is often as good as, and sometimes better than, the traditional hunting hours. Let's take a look at each of the three.

HUNTING PRESSURE

Anytime hunting pressure is a major factor dictating deer movement, you will find me in the woods during the midday hours. In most states you can count on significant hunting pressure during the opening weekend of the firearms season. Hunter activity keeps deer on the move more than normal, which is why many states achieve a very high percentage of the annual harvest on the first day or two of the season. Most of the deer killed during periods of heavy hunting pressure are taken as they attempt to evade other hunters. If you asked 100 hunters what were their favorite hours to hunt on opening day of the deer season, I'm sure that the majority would say the traditional hours of early morning and evening. My own records, which I have kept for 30 seasons, indicate that when pressure is a significant factor in deer movement behavior, the midday hours are nearly as good as the heralded early morning period and far better than the evening stint. My records show that I have taken 55 percent of the deer in the early morning hours, 40 percent at midday, and only 5 percent in the evening. Before going any further, perhaps we should clarify what the midday hours are. You may disagree with my assessment, but this is a good general timetable. The early shift is from legal shooting light until 10 A.M., the midday period is 10 A.M. until 3 P.M., and the evening shift is from 3 P.M. until the end of shooting hours.

It is probably no surprise to anyone that roughly half of the deer I've taken during these firearms seasons were taken during

When other hunters are on the move, sitting still can really produce.

the early morning period. All you have to do is sit back and listen to the gunfire on opening morning to figure out that activity is unusually high during this period. You are probably surprised, however, that I've taken nearly as many deer during the midday period. I'm not.

There are two very logical and yet very different reasons why the midday period is such an effective time to hunt where hunting pressure is significant. The most obvious is that hunter traffic tends to keep deer on the move, and a deer on the move is in trouble when the woods are full of hunters. A common scenario on opening day is for a hunter to walk to his stand just before shooting light and to remain on stand until late morning, by which time boredom, cold feet, lack of confidence, or all of the above will convince him that the best option is to do a little still-hunting. As only a fraction of the deer hunters in the woods today have the skill to still-hunt effectively, all our hunter really accomplishes is a walk in the woods.

This tends to disturb some deer, deer that very often end up in the sights of hunters who are sitting patiently on their stands.

After a little walk-about, our hunter meets up with his buddies, all of whom have been doing their own little walk-abouts, and they decide to head back to camp for a little lunch and a nap or perhaps put on a drive or two. Either way, the hunter waiting on stand is in the right place to take advantage. If the hunters return to camp for lunch and a power-nap, you can count on them disturbing a few deer once again when they return for the evening hunt. Multiply this activity by the number of hunters in the woods, and you can see why the midday period has produced nearly half of my deer when hunting pressure is a factor.

The flip side of the coin is that sometimes it is the absence of hunting pressure during the midday hours that encourages deer movement. I'll use my home state of Minnesota as an example. In the southeast part of the state where I live the firearms deer season begins with a nine-day-long bucks-only season held in early November. The rut is on, but hunting pressure is so heavy during the opening weekend that most rutting activity is confined to the hours of darkness. There are a few testosterone-crazed bucks that wander brazenly in search of a hot doe despite the number of hunters, but these bucks are the exception, not the rule. Most mature bucks put survival ahead of procreation. By Monday, most of the hunters have gone back to work. You will still have a few in the woods in the morning and again in the evening, but only a handful of die-hards stick it out all day. Those few that do often kill some mighty impressive bucks. Deer can sense when there are hunters in the woods and when there are not. They lay low mornings and evenings, but midday is time to make hay—or in this case, make little deer!

THE RUT

As the breeding phase of the rut nears, bucks spend more and more time on their feet cruising the countryside in search of the first receptive does, pawing out new scrapes, freshening existing scrapes, making rubs, and picking fights with other bucks. As the time for breeding draws near, you will see bucks chasing every doe they encounter. When a buck at last picks up the heady scent of that doe in estrous, he will put his nose to the ground and follow the scent trail until he finds her. Then he will follow her around like a love-struck teenager for a day or two until the job is done, and he wanders off in search of another receptive doe. All of that adds up to a lot of buck movement, and some of that movement is taking place at midday.

Early morning ranks first for buck activity during the rut in my book. After that first hour or hour and a half, things usually come to a standstill until late morning or just after the noon hour, when the action picks up for an hour or so. In fact, while looking back through my journals, I find that only rarely have I not seen deer while hunting the midday hours during the rut. This midday activity is usually followed by an afternoon lull. This is when I make use of the extra safety belt I carry in my fanny pack. I strap myself tight across the shoulders against the tree and try to grab a little nap. So far I have not been caught strapped to the tree by an approaching buck, but I suppose it is only a matter of time. The afternoon lull is hopefully followed by a flurry of activity around sunset.

I suspect that the midday hours are so predictably good during the rut for a couple of reasons. One, after a night of carousing, the bucks bed down shortly after full light for a much needed rest. By late morning or early afternoon, rested now and with that testosterone surging through their systems, the bucks have no choice but to get up out of their beds and go on with the rituals of the rut. Then, too, it is normal for bucks to get up at midday and browse a bit, relieve themselves, and get the kinks out.

The second reason is that few hunters bother to hunt through the midday hours. In my experience, lots of hunters talk about sitting in a stand all day, but few ever do. Bucks react to this vacuum by getting up and getting in on!

The Heater Body Suit is the best garment I have ever found for long stints on stand in cold weather.

LATE-SEASON FOOD STRESS

With many of the deer seasons across the Midwest and northern states now extending well into December and often January, hunters have an opportunity to hunt during a period when finding enough high-quality chow becomes the main focus of the whitetail population. The evening period typically provides the best hunting opportunity during the late season. Deer are often anxious to reach a food source and will vacate the bedding area in late afternoon to make the trek to the chow line. A stand overlooking the travel route or often the feeding area itself is a good choice.

While the last hour of shooting light is usually the best hour of the day during the late season, I also think that most hunters are missing out by not capitalizing on midday activity during these hunts. When conditions are favorable I've seen dozens of deer, including some good bucks, on their feet and chowing down at high noon.

Whitetail deer typically do a little snacking at midday. For most of the season, this midday feeding period does not offer much of an opportunity for hunters because the feeding period does not last long and the deer do not travel far from where they bedded, often only a few yards. But late in the season, with winter bearing down hard, whitetail deer instinctively know that they need to stoke that old internal furnace with some high-energy fuel at midday. The bucks, especially the big boys that have run themselves poor during the rut, are desperate to replace the body fat that disappeared in November. Without that fat reserve, a tough winter will spell doom for them.

Deer do not feed at midday every day during the late season. If it is very cold the deer will simply remain bedded to conserve energy. If the temperature is moderate there will be some midday activity. The very best midday late-season activity will take place on the first day of warmer weather after a winter storm. The longer the storm and severe cold have lasted, the more dramatic the midday activity will be. After being holed up for a day or two by a major storm, I've often seen dozens of deer feeding in open, wind-swept fields at midday, although don't expect mature deer to be so brazen.

This midday feeding period is not easy to take advantage of, and in some cases, trying to do so will only spoil what could be a good evening hunt, so you need to pick your time and place carefully. If you know where the deer like to lay up during the day and if you can slip in close undetected, the midday feeding period, which will take place within or on the perimeters of the bedding area, is definitely worth hunting.

Since, in most instances, I have found it impossible to slip into a stand close enough to the bedding area to be in good position to take advantage of the midday activity without alerting the deer to my presence, I usually opt for taking my stand before first light and sitting tight right through midday. I always figure that this strategy gives me at least two opportunities for action, one in early morning as deer slip into the bedding area and another at midday when deer get up to stretch, relieve themselves, and browse. You might think that sitting for five or six hours in low temperatures would be tough and I'll admit that before I began relying on a Heater Body Suit (contact them at 920-565-3273 or at heaterbodysuit.com) it often was, but this simple and effective garment takes the cold out of cold weather hunting.

My favorite way to take advantage of the midday feeding period is to slowly still-hunt through the cover the deer are frequenting. The problem with this is that no matter how good you think you are at sneak-hunting, you are going to disturb some deer along the way, so I only still-hunt areas where I am not counting on those same deer for my evening hunt. A few years back, I was using this tactic during Minnesota's late muzzleloader season. Several inches of wet, sticky snow had fallen during the night, the kind that clings to every branch and twig. All morning I sat on stand staring into that blank white world without seeing a deer. About 10:30, I hiked to a ridge thick with young aspen and began to slowly prowl through the heavy cover, taking only two or three steps at a time, stopping often to go to one knee to peer beneath the snow-laden branches. It was noon when I spotted him, or part of him anyway. Those brown, slender legs in a world of white gave him away. I could tell by the size and the color of the tarsal gland on his right hind leg that the deer was a buck. He was very close and coming closer. Already on my knees, I simply shifted the butt of the muzzleloader to my shoulder and waited. That buck is the only deer I have ever taken that had powder burns on his hide!

Pulling an all-day sit on stand is not for everyone. That is part of what makes an all-day sit so productive for those of us with the patience, stamina, and pure stubbornness to stick it out from dark to dark.

18

HUNTING EFFECTIVELY ON SMALL PLACES

I was not planning to include this chapter, but last evening as I was working on the book, a friend stopped by with some exciting news. He and his brother had just purchased 60 acres of land, most of it timber, in what we both know is a very good region for nice bucks. Like so many hunters today, my friend bought the land to hunt on. After my friend left, I got to thinking about all of the hunters I know who either purchase their own land for hunting or lease land on which to hunt. These are often small parcels and hunting them intelligently is not always easy.

I do not own any hunting land. I wish I did, but things have not worked out that way. However, a friend of mine did something very nice for me two years ago. This friend knew that I lived for bowhunting deer, especially big bucks. My friend had a friend with whom he had gone to school who owned a farm in one of the best areas in our part of the world for growing big bucks. My friend asked if I could hunt on his land. And that is how I came to hunt on this little farm.

Jim and Mary and their two small children live in a house on the land, but they work in town. Jim pastures a small herd of beef cows on the farm in the summer and takes enough hay off the two small alfalfa fields to see his cows through the winter months. A small stream that holds a smattering of both brookies and browns courses through the center of the property. Hardwood, mostly red and white oak, studs the sidehills, ridges, and cuts on the farm. Adjacent to their little piece of ground is a much larger farm on which I do not have permission to hunt. I've never seen another hunter on the other farm, but I know that someone hunts there because I hear his ATV going up and down the hills sometimes.

When my friend Tom first told me about the farm I was like a kid with a big package under the Christmas tree. I could not wait for Tom to join me, so I got directions to the farm and drove over one morning to do some snooping around. I hiked fast, sticking to the easily identifiable fenceline boundary and then began crisscrossing the interior of the property. In short order, I had seen it all and to tell you the truth I was disappointed. Not only was the farm small, just 80 acres, but every inch except the homestead and the two alfalfa fields was heavily pastured. If it would not have offended Tom, I would probably not even have bothered to hunt the farm. But I knew that Tom had gone out of his way to arrange for me to hunt there, so I vowed to hunt as hard as I could.

And I did. In fact, I hunted that little farm too hard. I put too much pressure on such a small piece of ground. I hung too many stands and moved those stands too often. I bumped deer feeding in the alfalfa fields on so many mornings as I hiked into my stand and again in the evenings as I returned to my pickup, that they got so they just kind of moved out of my way instead of running off. I hunted that 80 acres like it was 800 or 8,000. I hunted stupid that first season. Even with all of my mistakes, I still saw lots of deer, including some nice bucks, one of which I missed by a whisker when my arrow deflected off a single-strand electric wire fence between the buck and me. I could not hit that fence again with a thousand arrows! I also saw a monster buck. Saw him three times, in fact. Never close enough for a shot, though, as I saw him on neighboring property all three times. One time he crossed the county road and after I was done hunting I went to where he had crossed and studied his tracks. I often found those tracks on the little farm I hunted, so I knew that the big boy was snooping around some of the does that called the farm home.

All that winter, after the first season on the little farm was history, I scolded myself for being in such a rush, for overhunting the property, for not hunting intelligently as I knew I was capable of doing. I vowed to hunt smart the next year.

Every year when the big buck stories roll in, you can count on some real bruisers coming from small, often overlooked patches of ground.

I did a better job of it last season. Not perfect perhaps, but better, and sometimes improvement has to be enough. I took what I had learned that first season and put that information to work for me. Although I had set foot on nearly every square yard of turf on the farm, I did not overestimate my knowledge. Oh, I knew the farm well, but not nearly as well as the deer that lived there. A whitetail knows the 200, 300, 400, or 500 acres it calls home with the same familiarity an over-the-road trucker feels in the cab of his Peterbilt. I will never achieve that degree of intimacy with this piece of land, no matter how many years I am privileged enough to hunt it.

Most of my whitetail hunting is on big tracts of public land or large private farms and ranches. I like hunting these larger places, but I realize after two seasons of hunting that little farm that I hardly know them. I know them well enough to find my way back to the truck in the dark or if a fog rolls in and I know something about where the deer like to bed, where they eat, and where they go when disturbed, but even though I have hunted some of these places for many seasons, I do not know any of them as well as I know the land and the deer on that little farm in Wisconsin after just two seasons. That's the big advantage of hunting the same small piece of land season after season.

On larger tracts of whitetail habitat, I tend to take in only the general features of the land. I don't get a real handle on how any individual deer conducts its day-to-day business. And when I'm hunting property where I have room to roam, it's much more difficult to stick with a stand when things are slow. I find I'm always thinking that I should be over the next ridge or down in the swamp or out in the pine thicket.

Conversely, on my little farm, because my stand options are limited, I tend to stay put and because I give these stands time to produce, I see more deer.

HUNTING SMART

One of the things I did wrong during my first season on the 80-acre farm was hunting it too often. The reality is that no matter how careful you are in going to and from your stand, when you only have 80 acres to work with, there is a good chance that some deer are going to see or hear you. Add in the times that you get picked off on stand, and pretty soon every deer on the property has your number.

During my second season I hunted the farm exactly half as many days as I did the first season—and saw nearly twice as many deer. There are two big reasons for this dramatic increase in sightings. Because I was not spooking deer as often and tipping my hand with all of my comings and goings as I had done the previous year, the deer were more inclined to move naturally. The second reason was that I was real fussy about when I hunted.

The first year, I hunted the farm whenever I had a chance. The second year, I only hunted the farm when conditions were in my favor. To be more specific, I concentrated my efforts during three key periods. Actually, I would have hunted the farm the first day or two of the archery season, but I was off chasing elk in the Gilas of New Mexico. When I got back from that trip in early October, it was tempting to dash right over, but I resisted the urge. Early October is a tough time to find a good buck. The late summer/early autumn pattern, which is pretty dependable, is over and bucks tend to spend most of the night pigging out and the days just lying around being lazy. I've noticed over the years, as have other students of buck behavior, that there is a three- to four-day burst of activity towards the end of the second week in October, specifically October 11 to 14 here in the upper Midwest. Mature bucks will do a lot of rubbing and scraping during this brief stretch. Although I have never seen any scientific data to back it up, I believe that some of the oldest does come into estrous during this brief period. Maybe it's nature's way of insuring that the best mothers get bred, but that's just a hunch. All I know is that there will be a flurry of buck activity on these dates. I hunted three of these four days on the little farm and saw eleven bucks.

After that short stint I held off until early November. I probably would have hunted the farm some during the last week of October when the bucks were scraping strongly, but I was busy trying to find a good one out in Montana. When I got home I hunted the farm every day between November 6 and 11 and saw bucks each day. My best day was November 7, when I had five bucks into my decoy, the fifth buck being the largest at which I have ever flung an arrow, the same buck I had seen three times the previous season.

My last hunts on the farm were during the week of Christmas, when we had a brief dose of good old-fashioned winter. There was

There is a special sense of accomplishment when you take a deer from ground you know well.

enough snow and cold temperatures to make the alfalfa fields attractive, and I spent several days hunting near them. I saw a lot of deer and a number of bucks, but not the buck I was looking for. As I trudged back to my truck on that last evening, I realized that the little farm, the same piece of ground I had nearly given up on only a year earlier, had become one of my favorite places in all the world to hunt whitetail deer.

BUCKS IN THE SUBURBS

Over the years, it has been my privilege to travel extensively to hunt whitetail deer. Some of those hunts have taken me to wild places— wilderness. How do I describe wilderness? To me, the true measure of wilderness is when you can no longer hear the presence of man. There are places here in the states, such as the northern reaches of Michigan, Minnesota, North Dakota, Wisconsin, Maine, and Montana, where it is still possible to hunt a full day and, other than the occasional jet passing overhead, never hear a manmade sound. I've also spent many long days on stand in the forests of western Canada when the croaking of ravens, the chitter of pine squirrels, and the "popping" of aspen trees in the bitter cold were the only sounds to keep me company. Wilderness all.

I could not help but think about those places and the "sound of silence" as I perched in my stand in the good doctor's backyard. I found myself straining so hard to hear the crunch of leaves over the din of the neighbor's lawnmower, the hedge-trimmer up the street, the laughter of children playing in a park, and the insistent yipping of a neurotic, pampered dog, that I was giving myself a doozy of a headache.

Wilderness this ain't, I thought to myself.

I also thought about climbing down and going home. This suburban hunting didn't seem to fit my style. Then I heard something different amidst the din. I looked in the direction from which the sound had come and saw four gray ghosts slipping through the neighbor's backyard and headed my way. The deer paid no attention to the noises that had just moments ago so irritated me. But when a UPS truck came down the cul-de-sac behind which I perched, the lead deer, one of those old, long-necked, super-cautious, mature does, skidded to a halt and the other deer followed suit. This was a sound different from those she heard every day, something worth worrying over. The UPS driver pulled up in front of one of the homes, shut down the engine, ran to the house with his delivery, jumped back in his truck, started it, and went tearing up the hill. The doe and her tribe stood stone-still the whole time. When the UPS truck was gone, the doe flicked her tail and the string of deer continued marching in my direction.

In my pocket were two antlerless-deer-only tags and one either-sex tag. As in most suburban deer hunting situations, controlling herd numbers was, at least in the thinking of the city officials, landowners, and DNR, the most important consideration. I was more than willing to assist with the problem, but I must admit that as the string of four deer drew nearer my stand, I found myself sneaking a little peek behind them now and then to make sure that a buck was not tagging along. None were, so I turned my full attention to the old doe and her family. Two trails wove through the three acres of maple, basswood, oak, and green ash on which I hunted. One passed 30 yards above my stand, the other half that distance below. The deer took the lower trail and when they were screened from my view by a massive, toppled oak, I drew the Mathews and waited. My intention was to take the old doe, but evidently she had stopped to nibble a few of the wrinkled leaves that still clung to the branches of the fallen oak. The first deer to step out was a slightly smaller doe, probably one of the older doe's offspring from the previous year—not that it mattered to me or the arrow that sliced cleanly through her lungs. All four deer wheeled and ran back the way they had come, but only three made the neighbor's property.

Moments later, I knelt beside the fallen deer and affixed one of my tags to a rear leg. Then, without gutting the deer, I dragged it to a spot along the driveway to the doctor's home where I could easily load it into the back of my pickup truck. I stopped to register the deer, drove the ten miles to my own home, winched it up in my garage, skinned it, and boned out the carcass. Then I took the carcass to a small local zoo where the caged wolves, bears, cats, and coyotes would make short work of what was left.

On the drive home, I reflected on my first hunt for suburban deer. The barking dogs, laughing children, neighbors mowing, and all of the other comings and goings of life in the suburbs were distracting to me, there was no denying that. But when the deer had appeared on the scene, it was as if the outside world did not exist. The hunter in me took over and my total focus was on the deer and preparing myself mentally and physically for the shot.

I will admit that the shot worried me. Like most bowhunters, I always try to put the arrow into a vital location for a quick, clean kill, but I'll have to admit that I try even harder when hunting the suburbs. The last thing in the world we need as hunters is for a deer with an arrow sticking out of its butt to go blasting through a schoolyard or a backyard picnic. That is why I refuse to take any shot outside of my personal "gimmee" range when hunting in the suburbs. Nor will I take any shot other than a perfect broadside or slight quartering angle. If I can't get both lungs, I forget the shot. No exceptions.

In an ever-increasing number of suburban hunting situations, hunters are asked to take proficiency tests before they are issued permits to hunt. In some cases, local bowhunter groups conduct the tests, other times it is left to the local law enforcement officials. I know of hunters who balk at taking these tests, insisting that they are

Hunting small places close to home means that there might be time for a youngster to join you after school for an evening hunt.

an "infringement of their rights." I figure most of these whiners just can't shoot.

Hunting in the suburbs—literally in someone's backyard—is not a right, it is a privilege. It is a privilege we will lose if we allow a few slob hunters to ruin it for all of us.

FINDING A PLACE TO HUNT

That the suburbs are full of deer is no secret. But how do you go about finding a place on which to hunt those deer? Most suburban landowners are not just going to grant you permission to hunt if you come knocking on their door. You need an "in."

Paying attention has opened a lot of doors for me. When my family and I are at school, sports, church, or social functions, I always have one ear tuned for picking up on any conversation involving deer. Often that conversation is not about hunting but about how the deer are eating up the garden, the flowers, and those expensive new shrubs and saplings. This is when a courteous request to bowhunt from someone they know, dressed in street clothes or Sunday-go-to-meeting duds instead of camouflage, is likely to be greeted with an, "Oh, please, could you?"

I'm not ashamed to admit that I use my kids as scouts, too. I've gained access to some prime suburban hot spots over the years when one of my daughters has tipped me off to the fact that the parents of one of her friends are really upset with the marauding whitetails in their backyard.

If you don't have an "in," try what I call the "official route." This involves contacting city, county, or township officials and inquiring into the availability of any special hunts in the suburban areas of their jurisdiction. Many communities have special draw hunts to help manage deer herds. Often, these hunts are not well publicized and are not found in the general state hunting synopsis. You have to ask.

Even if there are no special hunts available, just letting these officials know that you are interested in hunting in their area may help to open the door for you. When one of their constituents is hounding them to do something about the deer problem, your name could easily be inserted into the conversation.

Conservation officers are another great resource to utilize. Convince the local C.O. that you are a responsible, legal, and ethical bowhunter and odds are excellent that he or she can put you on some property where he has been receiving complaints that deer are doing damage.

You may be saying to yourself, "Yes, that is all good information, but doesn't every hunter do all of those things?" The answer is an emphatic no. Most hunters know that there are lots of deer in many suburbs, but because they *assume* that all of the good hunting is already tied up, they don't even attempt to gain access. This bodes well for hunters with enough gumption to work at gaining access to suburban hot spots.

After years of hunting the suburbs, I can assure you that competition from other hunters is much greater on public land, and even on much of the private farming land in my area, than it is in the suburbs.

SCOUTING AND HUNTING THE SUBURBS

Because most suburban landowners are going to own anywhere from just a few acres up to perhaps 40 acres, scouting is pretty easy. My first step is to determine the property boundaries. Then I hike the property, looking for the usual sign: tracks, trails, rubs, scrapes, beds, and droppings. You can learn a lot about the habits of the deer that use or travel through the property from the landowners themselves. For instance, if Bob and his wife inform me that they rarely see any deer on their property during the day but see them nearly every evening in the little orchard at the far end of their property, I can be pretty sure before I ever put a foot down that I am looking at a deer coming to feed situation. But if Joe and his wife tell me that they often jump deer on their property in the middle of the day while out cutting wood or just enjoying their woodlot, I can assume that some deer are bedding on Joe's property. In other instances you will find that deer just travel through the property on their way to bedding and feeding areas. Determining which of these three situations exists will determine when and how I hunt the property.

If deer are traveling through the property to go to and from their food source and bedding areas, which is the most common scenario you will encounter on suburban property, setting up a stand or two along the main deer trail and occupying that stand during the first and last couple of hours of light is a no-brainer, made even easier by the fact that because habitat is limited in suburban situations, all the deer tend to follow one or two heavily-used trails, especially through any necked-down areas.

If the deer are feeding on the property on which you have permission to hunt, evenings will be your best bet. Trying to slip into your stand in the morning will only spook the deer on the typically tight quarters. Remember this when it comes to food sources. Because we are talking small parcels here, no food source is going to last the entire season. When you find deer feeding on fallen acorns, apples, or the landowner's garden, get on them quick and hunt them hard, because within a short time the deer will have consumed the groceries and moved on to someone else's backyard.

In my experience, it is rare to locate suburban property on which deer bed. The reason is that most parcels are too small and have too much human activity. Many times, deer that thrive in the suburbs bed on secluded parcels such as city or county parks, or any large parcel of land that does not get a lot of traffic. When the sun begins to set these deer filter out into the suburbs in their never-ending quest for food. However, if you are fortunate enough to gain permission to hunt a piece of property on which deer are bedding, my advice is to hunt it very, very carefully. Don't set up right in the bedding area, no matter how tempting. Instead, haunt the fringes and try to catch the deer coming and going. By hunting smart you can milk a whole season's worth of action out of a prime bedding area.

DON'T FORGET THE THANK YOU

When I am granted permission to hunt on suburban property, I make sure that I show the landowner how much I appreciate it. I do not make a pest of myself, but a few packages of fresh walleye fillets, maybe some nice venison chops, a smoked turkey, or a flowering plant if I notice that the family enjoys flowers, goes a long way towards being welcomed back the next year. You would be surprised how often these gestures, along with a card of thanks, help to open other doors in the neighborhood.

I'll be the first to admit that the suburbs are not as aesthetically pleasing to hunt as some of the other places in which I pursue whitetail. But having places to hunt within minutes of home where I am almost guaranteed to see deer is worth putting up with the noise and distractions of civilization.

19

GROUND BLINDS

What, you might ask, is a chapter on ground blinds doing in a book called *Treestand Hunting Strategies?* The answer is that the purpose of this book is to help you see more deer, have better shots at the deer you do see, and hopefully have more opportunities at good bucks. Most of the time, hunting from a treestand will afford you the best chance to do all of that. There are, however, situations when a ground blind is a better option than a treestand.

Such a situation presented itself just a few months before I sat down to begin writing this book. In fact, it was while discussing that particular hunt with this book's editor, Jay Cassell, that the two of us decided to include a chapter on hunting from ground blinds. My old friend Bill Jordan had invited me to come to northeast Montana to bowhunt the plentiful whitetail that call the Milk River home and to get some good video footage. Having hunted the Milk before, I quickly accepted the invitation, and during the third week of September, I joined Bill, John Dudley from Mathews Archery, and Don Kisky, an excellent young hunter and video producer from southern Iowa. The four of us and our four cameramen all headquartered out of the comfortable ranch home of our hosts, Terry and Donna Korman.

Normally, patterning a whitetail deer is a tremendous challenge because the deer live most of their lives in timber where they are not easily seen, so you end up trying to pattern a buck more by the sign he leaves behind than by actual visual observation. This is not the case, however, when hunting river-bottom deer in the West. The deer are pretty much confined to the willows, osier, Russian olive, and cottonwood trees that provide bedding cover along the banks of rivers and tributaries. They spend most of the daylight hours in the river-bottom cover and then venture out into the surrounding fields, mostly alfalfa in the case of the Milk River herd, to feed in the evening. After feeding off and on all night, they mosey back into the protective cover along the river banks with the rising sun. Patterning these deer is as close to easy as you will find in the world of whitetail hunting. The best way to accomplish it is to perch on a high hill for an evening to see where the deer are exiting the river bottom and which fields they are hitting the hardest. The first morning of the hunt you also want to be situated on a prominent bluff so that you can see deer exiting the fields and entering the cover. Then you can go in during the middle of the day and hang stands in the spots you have pinpointed as prime locations.

On our first morning, we all split up and headed for various vantage points so that we could watch over as much of the river bottom as possible. Everyone saw deer, including some nice bucks, but one very special buck caught the eye of Don Kisky and his cameraman, Glen Garner. At first, in the poor pre-dawn light, Don and Glen thought they were looking at a buck with incredible mass to his antlers, but as it grew lighter they realized that the buck's antlers were still sheathed in velvet, even though all of the other bucks were clean. The buck instantly became known in camp as the Velvet Buck, and Don and Glen concentrated all of their efforts for six days of hunting on taking him. The buck was feeding in an alfalfa field known as "The Pea Patch," and he was more predictable than any big buck I've ever seen. Every evening Don and Glen got to watch the Velvet Buck, sometimes from 100 yards away, sometimes 75, and once as close as 50 yards, but never within Don's comfortable shooting range. It got to be kind of comical really. Don and Glen would watch the buck walk out under a certain tree, so they would hang a stand in that tree and be perched there the next evening, only to have the buck walk out into the field at a different location. So they would hang a stand at that location, only to watch the buck walk out at a different spot, or maybe even under one of their vacated stands. They even went so far as to use a boat to slip in on the backside of the field so that they could easily access a couple of stands they had hung for morning hunts. They saw that buck on each and every hunt for six straight days, but never were able to get a shot.

When Don and Glen had to head for home, Bill asked if I could stay on for a couple of extra days and hunt the Velvet Buck. I quickly made the arrangements. He was not a real high scoring buck, but he was certainly a mature deer and a unique trophy and I was looking forward to trying my luck with him.

The next morning, after the deer had all retreated into the timber along the river bottoms to bed down for the day, Bill, my cameraman, Mark Womack, Bill's cameraman, Nick Mundt, and I slipped into the field where the Velvet Buck fed each evening and positioned a couple of the big round bales that were scattered about the field to make a natural ground blind. I had used round bales as blinds on a couple of occasions in the past and had found them to be very effective. Deer are accustomed to them and even if you relocate two or three to make a ground blind, they do not seem to notice. Mark would occupy a treestand 40 yards behind the hay bale blind on the edge of the timber to capture all of the action on film. If the plan worked, it would make for some unique whitetail hunting footage.

That afternoon, even though I had showered in the morning, I took another shower, put on clean underclothing, and my Scent-

My "shooting port" in the round bale ground blind.

Lok clothing. When I crawled into my hay bale blind, I sprayed all of my outer clothing and my bow down with Scent-A-Way spray. You might think that I go a little overboard on odor control, but I believe that fooling a mature whitetail's nose is the most critical aspect of any deer hunt and I knew that in this instance I was likely to have numerous does, fawns, and small bucks very near my blind before the Velvet Buck made his appearance. If this proved to be the case, I was going to need all of the odor control I could muster. As I alluded to in the earlier chapter on odor control, I'm glad I took all of those precautions, because two deer, a fawn, and a pretty nice nine-point buck actually ate some of the alfalfa off my blind without picking up my scent.

It was hot in the blind as I waited for the Velvet Buck to make his appearance, but when the first deer (a small band of does and fawns) entered the field, I focused all of my attention on making sure that they did not detect me and instantly forgot my discomfort.

More deer slowly filtered into the field. When a pair of immature ten-point bucks and the heavy-antlered nine point that would eventually munch hay right off my blind ambled into the Pea Patch, I started looking hard for the Velvet Buck because he was often in the company of that little bachelor group of bucks. Ten minutes went by, 20 minutes, and still no Velvet Buck. The sun was sliding low in the west, casting long shadows across the field, when the big-bodied buck with the antlers still sheathed in velvet finally made his appearance. I had not been able to see him, but Mark told me later that he had been hanging back just inside the timber, munching on chokecherries and taking his own sweet time before venturing out into the field. Mark had been filming the buck, much of it right under his treestand, for a half-hour before I ever laid eyes on him. He walked out into the field, and within minutes I was standing over the fallen buck. Once again, a ground blind had been the answer.

In case you are curious as to why the Velvet Buck had not shed his velvet at such a late date (September 24), the reason was obvious when I checked out the buck. His testicles were each about the size of a salted-in-the-shell peanut, and the buck simply did not produce enough testosterone in his system to cause the velvet to dry up like it does on most deer. Perhaps the buck had been born with abnormal testicles or some illness accompanied by high fever when the buck was a fawn had retarded their growth. Whatever the reason, the buck would never shed his velvet like other bucks and probably would not participate in the rut or breeding activities. Biologists have since told me that the buck would shed his antlers like other bucks and grow a new set in the summer, but that each new set would always be sheathed in velvet.

I'm a big fan of hunting from treestands and probably spend more time perched in a tree than some birds. But I'll be the first to admit that there are circumstances that make a ground blind a better choice than a treestand—and sometimes the only choice. For instance, in Michigan, treestands are not allowed during the firearms season. In addition, many hunters are either physically incapable of climbing into a treestand or have no desire to do so. There are also instances when there are no trees suitable for climbing in the spot you want to hunt. When I encounter these situations, I do not hesitate to abandon my accustomed lofty perch and do my hunting on *terra firma*.

Ground blinds can be broken down into three types: natural ground blinds, portable blinds, and semi-permanent ground blinds.

Natural ground blinds are usually abundant in the places the whitetail calls home. A deadfall, big stump, log pile, old rock wall or foundation, or maybe just the trunk of a big tree will all work as long as you sit still. You can enhance any natural ground blind by piling a few branches around to help break up your outline and cover any movements you might make. Some hunters carry a few yards of camouflage cloth in their packs to enhance the natural cover. A

With good camouflage, it does not take much natural cover to make a good ground blind.

lightweight folding stool makes any natural ground blind a more comfortable proposition. This type of blind played the starring role in my shortest successful bowhunt.

I had stopped by my buddy Fitzy's place to see if he wanted to join me that evening, but he was not feeling very well that day, so he told me to go on without him. As I left, I jokingly told Fitzy that I would be back with a buck before supper. He laughed and I hopped in my pickup and drove about three miles to a small woodlot where I had permission to hunt. I had two stands already in place in the woodlot, a fixed-position stand for me and a ladder stand for Fitzy. Both were good stands for the southerly breeze that had been blowing all day, but when I stepped out of the pickup I could feel that the wind was switching. Rain was forecast for that night and the wind was swinging hard to the east. Neither stand was good for an east wind, so I abandoned that plan and decided to just hunt from the ground on the far side of the woodlot. I found a deadfall lying up against the trunk of a mammoth oak that would provide good concealment. With just a few snips of my ever-present ratchet clippers I cleared the few branches that might interfere with my being able to draw my bow. I nocked an arrow and hung the bow from a branch stub while I put on gloves and a release and tugged on a face mask. I dug out my grunt call, gave a few contact grunts, and leaned back against a sturdy branch to wait. A slight noise behind me caught my attention, and I turned slowly to see an eight-point buck just slipping out of a field of standing corn and into the woods. It was obvious from the way the buck was looking for something that he had heard the grunts and was coming to investigate. When the buck stepped behind a clump of trees that blocked me from his view, I stood, grabbed my bow, and turned slowly. The buck just kept walking slowly in my direction, stopping every few steps to search the area, trying to find the buck he had heard grunt, I suppose. When the buck stepped behind the big tree against which my deadfall was wedged, I drew and waited for the buck to step out the other side. The range was about five yards. The sharp broadhead did a quick number on the buck. I dressed him out, put my tag on him, and dragged him the short distance to my pickup. Fitzy about keeled over when I pulled into the driveway, well before supper, with the buck in the bed of the pickup.

Natural ground blinds are effective because there is nothing out of place to catch the attention of the deer. If something is different or if something is missing, they will know it and their attention will be drawn to that spot. With a natural ground blind everything is, as the name indicates, natural, so there is nothing odd to draw attention.

Portable blinds also have a place in whitetail hunting. I have used two different types with good results. One is a Hunter's Specialties Collapsible Super Light Blind. This blind folds up to only 14 inches long and weighs next to nothing, so I can put one in my fanny pack or day pack and forget about it until I need it. The spun-

There are several lightweight portable blinds that will work well for either the archer or the gun hunter.

bonded nylon camouflage material is die-cut to give it that leafy look. Just jam the stakes in the ground around you and the 27-inch-high camouflage material provides excellent concealment for a hunter sitting on the ground. Actually, I use mine more for turkey hunting than I do for deer hunting, but there have been a half-dozen times when I have sure been glad I had it with me.

The other portable blind I use is a pop-up blind. Mine happens to be from Double Bull, but there are other types on the market. I've had mixed results with it. You can't just set the blind up anywhere and expect deer to ignore it, because they will not. A blind in the open will catch their attention every time. For best results, I like to tuck the blind back into some kind of cover and then use natural vegetation to further enhance the naturalness of the blind. All of this is much more critical for the archer than for the rifle hunter. Bruce McKenzie, an excellent whitetail outfitter in northern Alberta, routinely uses pop-up blinds for his guests when hunting the cutlines that dissect the Canadian bush country. The blinds are usually set up on top of a hill that provides a good view in both directions. The hunter sits in a folding chair, his rifle propped in front of him, with a small propane heater at his disposal. In this type of situation the pop-up blind is as much for protection from the elements as it is for concealment. I was amazed to see several deer that I did not shoot cross the cutline within 50 yards of my blind without paying any attention to it at all, or at the most giving the blind a cursory glance and then going on about their business as if the blind did not exist. In my experience, this simply does not happen here in the states, where the deer are hunted much harder than those in northern Alberta.

Sometimes I have been hunting in places where I have been able to leave my Double Bull blind set up in the same position for days or even weeks. Eventually, deer do accept the blind as part of their environment. The acceptance period seems to be shorter if I take advantage of natural cover to help camouflage the blind.

Permanent or semi-permanent ground blinds are very common in some parts of the country. For instance, if you book a hunt in Saskatchewan there is an excellent chance that you will find yourself hunting from a wooden or plastic box blind. These boxes are sometimes built on stilts or propped up on bales for a bit of elevation, but most of the time they just sit right on the ground. They are spartan, consisting of nothing more than a small doorway, a folding chair to sit on, and a long, narrow opening on one or more sides that you look through and, hopefully, shoot through when the time comes. If it is really cold, your outfitter will probably provide you with a portable propane heater. Spending a few days in one of these box blinds will test your patience and endurance and is a sure way to determine whether or not you suffer from claustrophobia. Obviously, these blinds are designed with the rifleman in mind.

The fanciest permanent ground blind I've ever hunted from was on a bowhunt in Michigan. It was a little log cabin about ten feet long, five feet wide, and just tall enough that I could stand stooped over without banging my head on the ceiling, but plenty high enough to enable me to draw my bow while either seated or kneeling. Inside was a very comfortable chair, a stack of magazines and books, a cooler with cold drinks, and a portable heater, although when I hunted from the blind in early October, the heater was not necessary. There were three camouflaged viewing and shooting windows, all of which opened without the faintest squeak by simply pulling them towards you to create an 18-inch by 18-inch shooting port. Twenty yards in front of the little cabin blind was the biggest pile of carrots and sugar beets I had ever seen. It happened to be my first experience with hunting over bait and I was not prepared for the prodigious quantity used in that region. I found out later that the reason so much bait is used is that everyone is trying to outdo their neighbor in drawing the most deer to their bait. Quite frankly, it was not my kind of hunting, but it was interesting to watch the deer, racoons, and porcupines feed on the bait, all of them seemingly oblivious to the little log house, which I was told had been in that same location for seven years.

The key to a permanent ground blind is to have it in position long enough that the deer just accept it as part of the surroundings, or to have it far enough away from where you expect to see deer that it does not pose a threat to them.

I know hunters who are so into hunting from treestands that they refuse to hunt from the ground. This is a mistake, because there are definitely situations when a ground blind is a better option than a treestand.

20

STRANGE STANDS

I usually hunt the same kinds of stands you do, ladders, climbers, fixed-position, or ground blinds. But over the years I have found myself occupying some unusual stands, as well.

Once, while hunting the late muzzleloader season down in southern Iowa, I found an out-of-the-way harvested cornfield tucked back in a little valley. A quick inspection for tracks plainly showed that a number of deer were visiting the picked cornfield on a regular basis. It was bordered by heavy timber on three sides. On the fourth side was a deep ditch grown up to weeds, brush, and scrub trees, mostly stunted willow and box elder. These ditches, caused by erosion, are common in southern Iowa, northern Missouri, western Illinois, and probably in other places I have not hunted, as well. A generation or two of farmers had been discarding old machinery in that ditch. The grain hopper of a long-out-of-commission John Deere combine became my stand the next day. It was pretty comfortable and the rim of the grain hopper provided a nice rest for my muzzleloader. As the wind picked up in late morning ahead of an approaching storm, I was glad for the protection of the steel walls of the hopper. A pair of field mice, cute little buggers with white feet and long whiskers, had a nest somewhere in that hulk of a rusted combine. Their route to the outside world was up through the hole in the bottom of the grain hopper. Then, seemingly without effort, they would scamper up the steel walls and disappear over the edge. Sometimes in minutes, sometimes longer, they would tip back over the edge with their little cheeks crammed with seeds for their winter cache. They were leery of me at first, but when they discovered that whatever the big orange blob in the hopper was it obviously meant them no harm and even left tidbits of peanut butter sandwich and sugar cookie for their enjoyment, they pretty much accepted me as just another old, rusty piece of machinery, which I am sorry to report is becoming a more accurate description with each passing year. By the end of the day the mice had found that it was easier to scamper up my leg and over my shoulder to get out of the hopper than it was to scale the rusted, steel walls.

I never did shoot a deer from that combine hopper. I sat in it all day because, as I mentioned, there was a winter storm brewing and I

The hopper of this old combine made a fine stand one day in Iowa.

figured deer would be tanking up on groceries prior to the storm. They were. My journal indicates that I saw 23 deer that day, but none were the caliber of buck I sought. I tend to get real fussy when hunting places with the trophy potential of southern Iowa. Years before, however, I did take a little buck with my bow while perched on another old combine in an abandoned grove in southern Minnesota. That one, as I recall, was an old Minneapolis Moline and if any mice called it home they kept to themselves. I've pressed other farm machinery into service as temporary stands over the years. Ever hear of a car called a Whippet? I hadn't either until I sat in a windowless specimen that just happened to offer a perfect view of a brushy fenceline that connected with the abandoned grove in which the old car rested. My buddy Larry Weishuhn killed a dandy Iowa buck from the box of an empty corn wagon a few years ago when we were hunting together, and just this past season I took a stand for a couple of evenings in an old manure spreader that had conveniently been discarded 20 yards from a heavily-used creek crossing. (When I mentioned to my father-in-law that I was hunting from a manure spreader, he commented that somehow he found that fitting.)

A real shocker for a Minnesota boy was when I made my first trip to South Texas to hunt and found myself sitting in a bass boat seat on the specially-rigged top of a Chevy Suburban. The driver slowly drove down the ranch roads, or *sendearos*, as they call them down in that country, while you looked for deer from the elevated perch of the Suburban. When you spotted a deer you pushed a button with your foot that set off a buzzer in the cab and signaled the driver to stop. It was unique, perfectly legal in Texas, and I'm sure effective, but it was not my style. I asked if I could just take off and wander through the prickly pear and mesquite and do some rattling. The driver of the Suburban looked at me like I had lost my marbles, but he turned me loose and I ended up taking a nice buck and did not have to write a thank-you letter to Chevrolet.

Down in Texas they don't think this is strange, but I sure did.

On another occasion, a friend named Cuz Strickland and I were bowhunting a place that Mossy Oak has in Alabama called Lee Haven. A character by the name of Spence Bonjean runs the place, and he had spent the first night in camp telling ghost stories to those of us huddled around the old kitchen table. These were not your run-of-the-mill ghost stories, they were about a ghost that inhabited the old house in which we were staying. Whether or not you happen to believe in ghosts, all I can say is that the evidence, which had been gathered over a century or two, pointed strongly towards the existence of this one. It seemed to me that there were more lights left on in that house after everyone finally went to bed than is normal in a deer camp.

I'm not quite up to admitting that all of that ghost talk had me spooked, so let's just say that after what I shall term a "restless" night, I got up, had a little breakfast, and was dressed and waiting for a ride to my morning stand well before the necessary hour. It was a warm, sultry morning, which is not uncommon in the Deep South during deer season. There was no hint of either moon or stars, what my grandpa used to refer to as a night as black as the inside of a cat. A soupy ground fog hung over everything. Spence dropped me off on the rutted trail and told me to follow the bright eyes until I came to a big, live oak. The stand was in the crotch of the oak. I did as instructed and was in the stand a long time before first light.

On mornings like that one, there is no such thing as the "break of day," dawn is more of an oozing process as the black of night grudgingly gives way to various shades of dirty gray. Although I tried to occupy my mind with other things, it seemed that all I could think of as I sat there in the black listening to screech owls carry on all around me was that damn ghost. I was relieved when enough light finally seeped into the night sky so that I could make out individual trees and could get down to the business of trying to lay eyes on a deer. A half-hour later, I looked straight down from my stand, on the opposite side of the live oak I had ascended that morning, and noticed what looked like a big hole in the ground. The hole was grown over with vines, but from the shape of it, rectangular and about six feet long by three feet wide and deep enough that in the poor light and fog I could not see the bottom, it had all of the characteristics of an open grave. I tried to keep my eyes scanning the thick vegetation surrounding my stand for some sign of a deer, but I'll admit I spent more time staring into that black hole beneath my stand than I probably should have. Maybe that is why I did not see any deer that morning.

I was to meet Spence back on the road where he had dropped me off at ten o'clock, so at about a quarter to the appointed hour, I climbed down from my stand and walked around the huge live oak for a closer inspection of that hole in the ground. I discovered some wrought iron fencing tangled up in the briars and vines and, beneath a skiff of forest duff, a moss-covered slab of stone that had to weigh a ton or more.

When Spence picked me up I asked him about the hole in the ground. "Oh, yes, I meant to mention that to you, but it slipped my mind," he said. Then he proceeded to tell me the story of how the son of the owner of the plantation had died of typhoid or something and had been buried in the grave beneath the live oak sometime in the early to mid 1800s, I have forgotten the exact year. The grieving parents had erected an ornate wrought iron fence around their son's final resting place and placed a four-inch-thick slab of engraved marble over the grave. After the Civil War, when there was severe and widespread poverty in the war-ravaged South, gangs of men would roam the countryside robbing graves, looking for any valuables that might have been buried with the deceased. Naturally, the graves of the wealthy were favorite targets. In the case of the open grave beneath my stand, the men had used a team of mules to slide the heavy slab of stone off the grave.

Spence and The Cuz both swear that it was merely a coincidence that I happened to be hunting that stand that morning, but I don't believe either one of them.

One January, while hunting the late muzzleloader season in Iowa, I found a small plot of soybeans that was being hit hard by deer. There were no trees suitable for a stand, so I improvised by using brush and limbs to build a ground blind on top of a grub pile the farmer had bulldozed up when clearing the plot. The next afternoon, when I slipped into my ground blind, it had warmed up substantially, and shortly after I settled in I heard a rustling and noticed a racoon slowly prowling along on the grub pile. I did not think much of it. Racoons often come out for a little snooping around when the weather warms during the winter months. But when it spotted me and then came directly at me, hissing and spitting like a mad cat, I became a little concerned. I stomped my foot to startle it, but that only seemed to make it more bold. As the racoon waddled into the blind with me, I grabbed a stick and took a swing at him. My aim was deflected by the brush and I only managed to clip his rump. He got the idea that he was not welcome, though, and backed out of my blind and disappeared down a hole a few yards away. The racoon's unusual behavior led me to believe that it was probably rabid. As I have this thing about long needles in the belly, I was concerned when a quick inspection of that grub pile revealed that it was riddled with holes just like the one the racoon had gone down. It's hard to concentrate on deer when you are waiting for a mad racoon to pull a sneak tunnel attack on you. The situation made me recall a few high adventures in Vietnam when we would discover one of the elaborate tunnel systems used by the Viet Cong and would have to go in and ferret them out.

A half-hour later I heard a hissing behind me and here came that racoon up through one of the holes. It was getting to be prime time for deer to show up and I did not want to make a commotion, so I just sat still and hoped the racoon would wander off, but no such luck. He made a beeline for my blind, hissing and spitting and snarling the whole time and hunching his back to make himself look bigger. I tried to reason with him and asked him to be a good racoon and leave me alone, but he was having none of it. When he was a few feet away I whacked him behind the ear with my stick and put him out of his misery. A few minutes later another racoon came crawling out of one of the holes and I could not help but think that some things, like me shooting a deer from that grub pile blind, for instance, are just not meant to be.

The spookiest stand I ever sat in was an abandoned ranch house in southeast Colorado. I was hunting with an outfitter buddy of mine by the name of Tom Tietz. Tom had told me about a monster whitetail that he called "the Outhouse Buck" because twice the buck had been jumped by ranch hands near the old outhouse on the abandoned homestead.

"The attic of that old house would make a great stand for that buck," said Tom, "but so far none of my hunters will go in there."

"If that buck is as big as you say, I'd sit a stand in hell for a crack at him," I said.

Deer become accustomed to abandoned buildings, and I have hunted out of a number of them over the years. Barns, graineries, and even old chicken coops are not bad, but there is something spooky about stepping into a long-abandoned house in the black of pre-dawn.

So Tom dropped me off in the black of pre-dawn the next morning, told me to follow a certain fenceline for a quarter-mile until it crossed a dry creek, and then to follow the creek north until I came to the abandoned ranch. "With this wind, you should hear it before you see it," Tom said. "The old windmill has an eerie creak to it."

A half-hour later I heard the rusted windmill complaining in the wind. Tom had been right, that windmill sounded like something out of an old Alfred Hitchcock movie. But it was not nearly as eerie as stepping through the door of the old ranch house. Critters, mostly small, but one with larger claws—probably a racoon or possum—went scampering everywhere when the beam of my little flashlight cast its weak glow over what had once been the living room of someone's home. I swallowed hard and started up what was left of the stairs leading to the attic. I gave some thought to going back outside until it got light, but I fought back my apprehension, reminding myself that I was a grown man who had survived a war and that there was nothing I should be afraid of in the old house. Still, it took everything I could muster up to climb those steps. Tom said the upstairs was an attic, but I think it was a bedroom because there were the remains of a bed in one corner, a broken bedside table, one of those metal wash basins, and a wooden kitchen chair strewn about. Now that I think about it, I'll bet Tom never did make it to the upper floor of that creepy old house.

Anyway, the wooden floor was covered with an inch of bat poop that did not make the place smell all that good and probably made the air less than healthy to breathe. As quietly as possible, which was not all that quietly since the floor boards creaked and groaned with every cautious step I took, I set the chair by the north-facing window, in which only one broken pane of glass remained.

It took forever to get light that morning. When it did, the bats began returning from their night of hunting and flew in the open window just over the top of my head. My wife and the girls would not have liked that much, but I did alright with the bats. There is not enough hair on my head anymore for them to get tangled in anyway. But when a screech owl that also called the old attic home came swooping in the window, it startled me so bad that I reared back and fell right off that wobbly, old chair. A dozen bats and that owl were all trying to get out the window at once and my fall caused a massive eruption of dust that darn near choked me to death. When I finally quit coughing and caught my breath, I picked myself up off of the floor and looked out the window just in time to see a white flag disappearing beyond the weed-choked remains of the corral.

INDEX